LETTING GO

Wave Goodbye To The Pain Of The Past | Say Hello To The Joy Of Now | Find Closure And Inner Peace | Let It Go And Move On

REBECCA COLLINS

CONTENTS

Disclaimer	v
Free Gift	vii
Introduction	ix
1. Why People Can't Let Go	1
2. The Art Of Forgiveness	10
3. Dealing With Painful Memories	20
4. The Mind-Body Dynamic	30
5. The Trigger Is The Gun	40
6. Forgive And Move On	53
7. Moving Into The Light	70
8. Love Yourself Deeply	89
Afterword	103
Sources	107
Notes	109

DISCLAIMER

The content contained within this book may not be reproduced, duplicated or transmitted without direct written permission from the author or the publisher.

Under no circumstances will any blame or legal responsibility be held against the publisher, or author, for any damages, reparation, or monetary loss due to the information contained within this book. Either directly or indirectly. You are responsible for your own choices, actions, and results.

Legal Notice:

This book is copyright protected. This book is only for personal use. You cannot amend, distribute, sell, use, quote or paraphrase any part, or the content within this book, without the consent of the author or publisher.

Disclaimer Notice:

Please note the information contained within this document is for educational and entertainment purposes only. All effort has been executed to present accurate, up-to-date, and reliable, complete information. No warranties of any kind are declared or implied. Readers acknowledge that the author is not engaging in the rendering of legal, financial, medical or professional advice. The content within this book has been derived from various sources. Please consult a licensed professional before attempting any techniques outlined in this book.

By reading this document, the reader agrees that under no circumstances is the author responsible for any losses, direct or indirect, which are incurred as a result of the use of the information contained within this document, including, but not limited to, — errors, omissions, or inaccuracies.

Copyright Rebecca Collins 2022 - All rights reserved.

ISBN: 9781915677174

FREE GIFT

Free for you. 10 Weekly Issues of Rebecca's life-changing newsletter "Reclaim Your Power" Rebecca covers Self Love, Self Esteem, Making Friends, Getting Your Life Back & Living A Life of Freedom.

https://rebecca.subscribemenow.com/

Scan with your smartphone's camera

INTRODUCTION

"The past has no power over the present moment."
–Eckhart Tolle

From the moment we come into this world, we begin to trail a thread behind us. This is our lifeline and as we go through each experience, the thread gets longer and longer. Often it gets knotted and tangled and, before we know it, the thread has turned into a very long cord that holds us tied to our past. Not only that, but it also weighs us down in our present.

We can't cut the thread as it is part of what makes us who we are and it isn't always easy to unpick all the knots that have built up over the years. But we can untangle those parts that are stopping us from moving forward in life.

When you cannot let go of things that happened to you in the past, they have a powerful hold over your emotional, psychological, and physical health. But what exactly does it mean to 'let go' and how can you do that?

It is never easy to forget the past, no matter what anyone tells you. And quite frankly, forgetting is not the answer because things stay buried deep within us even if we wished they didn't. If you want to move on in your life, you need to come to terms with whatever has gone on before and find peace within yourself. Only then can you look forward to a radiant future, free of regrets, pain, and old patterns of behavior.

Perhaps you are tied to a past in which you lost someone close to you or you suffered intense pain. Maybe you did something that left you feeling remorseful. Wishing things could have been different is not going to resolve how you feel now, but hoping for a better future will.

When I was growing up, I didn't have the best relationship with my father. He drank too much and could be very volatile when he did. He certainly wasn't a good role model for me or my siblings. Even when he became very ill, I couldn't bring myself to visit him because I was unable to forgive him.

Long after he died, I continued to wish my childhood had been different – that he had been a better father to us all. That made me unable to trust men, and I struggled to build strong relationships with anyone as I grew older. It took me many years to deal with those painful childhood memories and see things from a different perspective. To do that, I had to stop dwelling on my past experiences, release their hold on me, and focus more on how I wanted to live in the now.

You may have gone through something similar and even though you want to lead a full, happy life, those past experiences keep sabotaging that possibility. People around you might tell you to let go, but you keep on repeating the same thought processes and patterns of behavior, feeling tied to the thread that keeps pulling you backward. It can be frustrating, limiting, and even depressing.

In this book, I want to offer you some alternatives to that and help you to get free of the past. Instead of holding on to false beliefs about yourself, or allowing past events to manipulate your present, you can begin to release yourself and find happiness. You will find some practical exercises to help you work through your issues in each chapter and plenty of tips on how to handle your emotional ups and downs as they arise.

I'll be taking you through some of the reasons why it can be difficult to let go and offer you proven strategies to overcome that. We'll be looking at how important it is to forgive (yourself and others) and why your memories of what happened aren't always a reliable source. You will also discover more about the mind-body dynamic and find ways to release yourself from both mental and physical pain that stem from your past.

If you often find yourself triggered by something in your present, you will discover pointers on how to respond rather than react. And you can use the strategies that I feature based on recent scientific findings to cope with difficult emotions and behaviors that prevent you from being able to move forward.

You may find yourself in a very dark place at this moment. I want you to know that there is always light on the other side. To reach it, you have to keep moving. Stagnating in thoughts of what could have been and holding on to old negative emotions is not good for you. I know you want to be free of those, which is why you will find plenty of strategies in this book to help you.

The fear of letting go can be so terrifying that it often feels easier to stay trapped in painful memories and emotions. I know how that feels but it doesn't have to be that way.

Once you begin to let those bright shafts of light into your life, you will discover that it is possible to find fulfillment and happiness. Cut yourself some slack, loosen your grip on that tangled, knotted thread and relax. A new day is beginning and all you have to do is open up your eyes and reach for it.

Join me as we leave the darkness of the past behind us and step into the brightness of the future.

Can I ask a quick favor?

Would you spare me just 2 minutes to write an honest review for this book from wherever you bought it. Reviews mean such a lot to me. Thanking you in advance.

Rebecca x

1

WHY PEOPLE CAN'T LET GO

'People have a hard time letting go of their suffering. Out of a fear of the unknown, they prefer suffering that is familiar'. –Thich Nhat Hanh

As strange as it may sound, many of us cling to our past because it is what we know. We lived through certain experiences, things happened to us, and people affected us, and we are all too familiar with these things.

We believe that they define us, that they control our life now, even if the very thought of them makes us suffer. How can we possibly step so far outside of our comfort zone to face the unfamiliar? What lies beyond that and can we reframe our mental and emotional state of being in line with new perspectives?

Moving house

Think of it as moving house. At the moment, you live in a tiny, cramped apartment. It is full of clutter you have been accumulating for years – most of which you don't use or need. It's difficult to get around the place, have friends over, or even relax because it is so small, but it is home to you. It has a familiarity to it that reassures you, despite it being totally impractical.

Now, imagine moving to a newer, more spacious home – one where you can declutter, spread out, invest in some nice new furniture, have friends around, and feel less stressed. Doesn't that sound good? The only thing that might be stopping you is that fear of the unknown: What if you don't feel happy there? What if the neighbors aren't friendly? What if it is too big to keep tidy?

Such questions may seem silly because we would all like to live in a spacious new home, right? In effect, preferring to stay in the old cramped place doesn't make sense at all. And yet, we would rather stay there than face all of the discomforts of the unknown.

When you think about letting go of the past, it's exactly the same thing. Fear keeps us stuck there but familiarity makes us believe it is where we belong. Let me tell you now – it isn't. You belong somewhere where you can feel calm, relaxed, and joyful, and that is why moving on is so important.

You may fight fiercely to stick to your past because certain things mattered to you. You wish a certain person you loved hadn't left you and you hold on to that pain. You wish you hadn't been treated so badly by someone and you hold on to that anger. But clinging to things that we can no longer have just isn't good for us.

It's like trying to keep a bad cold and refusing any medication in the belief it will make you well. That simply doesn't work. Being stuck in a time warp also prevents you from enjoying what you do have in the here and now, or what you can have in the future.

I know the idea of letting go can be scary. It forces you to change, face uncertainty, and leave behind the comfortable or usual. As humans, our resistance to change is actually quite strong. We are hardwired to fight against it, with our amygdala interpreting change as a possible threat. This is a pair of small almond-shaped regions deep in the brain that help to regulate emotions and encode memories.

When the amygdala is activated, it releases the hormones crucial for the fight, flight, or freeze response. It's no wonder that we hold on to the past so tightly, even if it wasn't pleasant or fulfilling. The good news is that when we focus on the positive aspects of change, our psychological make-up changes to one of optimism and calmness. To reach that state, we need to focus on three things:

1. Our dissatisfaction with the way things are now
2. Have a positive vision of the future
3. Take concrete steps to make that vision a reality

It's not until we reach a certain level of discomfort that we can acknowledge that change is needed. Moving from your old house might be a big upheaval, but you have to go through that to start enjoying your new home. It can involve getting rid of items you no longer need, and giving up on things you thought you did need.

You have to clean, sort, and plan for the move before removal day comes. And when it does, it can be an extremely tiring experience. But once you find yourself sitting in your new home, you will feel like a different person.

So, are you stuck in the past? Here are some pointers to help you reach clarity about whether or not that is the case.

You carry a lot of resentment

Resentment is like carrying a ton of weight around with you that has grown over time. All of the perceived wrongs you feel you have been a victim of in your past turn into resentment, which is a heavy load to bear.

If you feel constantly under attack, are over-sensitive to criticism, or think other people are luckier than you, it can turn into a fixation. You replay old hurts like a sad playlist and just can't seem to forgive or forget.

Resentment will impact your life in the present, making you believe that if bad things happened to you in the past, they will happen again. If your partner cheated on you at some point, this will lead you to believe that a new partner will do the same.

If you were rejected for a new job position, you could think the same thing will happen when you go for the next job. It becomes a vicious circle of equating the past with the present and prevents you from achieving your full potential.

You wish you could change the past

Since time travel hasn't been invented yet, going back to the past to change something that happened to you simply isn't possible. If you have regrets and wish you had the opportunity to do things all over again, that is normal. We all do.

But fixating on missed opportunities and past mistakes can make you less motivated to get on with your life now, especially if your inner dialogue always tells you, "I wish this or that had/hadn't happened." While you are wasting all of your energy thinking about what could have been, your dissatisfaction with the present can be exaggerated and this stunts you in the long term.

You constantly compare the present to the past

If you find yourself comparing things from the past to what you have now, that is a clear sign that you are stuck in the past. Your relationship with your ex may be over, but if you are still comparing him/her with your present partner, that will not help to build a healthy relationship.

Maybe you regret leaving your neighborhood because your new one is not living up to your expectations or you keep comparing it with where you lived before.

This yearning for a time when things were better and you were happier can also keep you in a state of dissatisfaction about your present life and prevent you from embracing change. By focusing on a life you no longer live, how can you expect to enjoy your new one? Say goodbye to old memories of a past life and embrace the one you have now.

You fear major change

Sometimes, it's comforting to think about the past and quite healthy to feel a sense of nostalgia as you reminisce on happier times. You may recall with fondness your first love, or a favorite pet you had while growing up. But when these memories make you scared to love again, or even to get a new puppy, then your past is dictating your present.

Being in a constant state of refusing to change can make any new experiences frightening and stop you from trying them. But life is all about change and when we embrace it, we grow and find contentment.

If you can relate to any of the above points, it may be time to consider getting unstuck from your past. That doesn't necessarily mean forgetting your past loves, homes, pets, jobs, or anything else. What it does mean is bringing your attention to the present and looking at ways of enriching your life today. Letting go won't make you any less interesting as a person or rob you of your personality. Relinquishing anything from the past that is negatively affecting your present can be liberating, allowing you to be the person you always thought you were deep inside.

You will feel lighter, more at ease, and released from the pull of a past that you no longer need.

Here are things to consider when letting go of the past:

Resisting, suppressing, or fighting your emotions on a regular basis slowly uses up all of your energy reserves. The constant struggle between the past and the present is exhausting and can cause you to feel defeated and hopeless.

Letting go helps you to live in the moment and experience all the wonderful things around you. You will feel more present, engaged, and motivated as you reconnect with your authentic needs and desires.

Once you stop fixating on the past, a whole new future opens up to you. You will find yourself able to plan more effectively to achieve your goals and not be weighed down by past mistakes or failures. Eventually, you will become more comfortable with the idea of change and open yourself up to new possibilities.

When you release yourself of the heavy attachments to the past, you will be more able to enjoy a sense of freedom – the freedom to live as you choose. You still have your memories and nothing can change past events, but it will become easier for you to resist reacting to them when they pop up in your mind. At some point, you will reach a stage where you can observe them as they float by, like a dark cloud on a sunny day.

Freeing yourself from the past doesn't make you cold-hearted or uncaring. In reality, it frees you to be more accepting of others, less-judgmental, and more forgiving. You will develop the ability to love yourself more and forgive yourself for past mistakes without anxiety or guilt.

Letting go is about mentally releasing attachment to something. Instead of fighting for a person or thing to be in our lives, we let go of that need or desire and accept what is instead. Acceptance plays a key role here, and I'll be talking about that a little later on.

For now, I want you to begin by considering what thoughts, and feelings well up in you when you think about major markers in your past. How are they keeping you from moving on and how much are you prepared to let them go? Let's look at some negative emotions connected with your past that you might be experiencing:

- Anger
- Shame
- Low self-esteem
- Lack of confidence
- Jealousy
- Hate
- Self-disgust
- Insecurity
- Pessimism
- Sadness
- Grief
- Loneliness

Can you add any more?

Certainly, some people have undergone extremely serious events in the past that can have a massive impact on their psychological health. Post Traumatic Stress Syndrome (PTSD) is a recognized medical condition that requires specialized attention by a trained professional. If you are suffering from PTSD, you need to seek help and begin the journey of recovery.

Traumatic incidents can have long-lasting effects on the well-being of victims and are not to be shrugged off as just 'something that happened to me.'

This book focuses more on helping you to move on with your life when you feel burdened by regrets, painful experiences, longing for something or someone you have lost, or life changes that you cannot get used to.

It is about coming to terms with whatever happened, letting go of any attachments, and being able to appreciate the present. Life is way too short to do otherwise.

The process of moving on

When we decide to leave the past behind, it can often feel like going through a period of grief. This is because we pine for something we no longer possess. It could be your youth, your physical appearance, your career, or even the fact that your children have grown up and flown the nest.

It isn't always a dramatic event but it is usually a desire to reclaim something that has changed – something you were familiar and comfortable with. Letting go of anything is never easy, but the more we hold on to it, the heavier the burden can become.

You may be in denial, then feel angry, or try to rekindle what is no more. You could feel lost and not know how to handle your present life until you finally reach the point of accepting how things are.

Denial. When you are in denial, you are avoiding reality. If, for example, your partner leaves you for someone else, you could go to great lengths to convince yourself that there must be some mistake – that it isn't true. It is normal to go through this stage but if such an incident occurred years ago and you are still in denial, this is a kind of coping mechanism that is not serving its purpose anymore.

Anger. As you try to come to terms with your reality, it is natural to ask questions such as 'Why me?' or "What did I do wrong?' This leads to frustration and can make you feel angry. If, for example, your car was stolen, you may take it to heart.

The truth is that this kind of event is usually nothing personal – you were just in the wrong place at the wrong time. Your first reaction may be to deny it has happened, and then anger builds up inside, leaving you feeling bitter and incensed. While this kind of anger is usually short-lived, you might hold on to it for a long time after the event.

Bargaining. Irrational hope can be very destructive when the facts show otherwise. Although you may hold a torch for a previous partner who walked out on you and dream of 'what ifs', the reality is unlikely to meet your desires.

At this point, you could find yourself being prepared to accept someone back into your life who treated you badly or give someone another chance who clearly doesn't deserve it. You may make promises that if only things could go back to the way they used to be, you would become a better person or try harder. This kind of bargaining doesn't work and it will not be long before you need to move on to the next stage.

Depression. This is the stage where you feel that you have lost but haven't fully accepted it yet. It is when you realize that there's nothing you can do but you are not prepared to accept it yet. With my first example, you may find yourself in the depression stage, when you don't want to talk to anyone, spend most of your time crying and have a hard time eating.

Many people get stuck at this stage because they are not yet prepared to fully accept the reality they are dealing with. However, once they overcome this, they will find themselves feeling better as they have now come to the last stage, which is acceptance.

Acceptance. Acceptance means that you reach a stage of inner peace and are ready to get on with your life. This could be described as the most difficult stage of all, and it can take years to get to a place where you can finally accept reality. There are many things you can do to ease yourself through this process, which we will take a look at later on in this book.

Letting go isn't a one-off decision that you make. It is a change in your mindset that requires time and effort. Your patterns of thinking and behavior may be so ingrained that it feels normal to you to hark back to having the past as your point of reference – your ground zero.

Even when you try to break free of your past, issues will keep coming back to prevent you from moving forward. So, you have to be patient with yourself and not expect to wake up one morning and feel like a completely different person. You will always be the same person, but you can handle your thoughts and feelings differently.

In the process of letting go, you don't need to try to negate what you are feeling either. Just by acknowledging that you feel sad, angry, or insecure, that is a breakthrough in itself. If you are going through tough times, you might worry that you will always feel that way.

Once you embrace the impermanence of those negative emotions that crop up, it will be easier for you to reduce their power over your life today. Leave the past behind and free yourself to enjoy the present!

Key highlights:

- **Fear of the unknown can keep you locked in the past.**
- **Deciding to move on can seem harder than staying where you are.**
- **Our ability to change can only be successful when we acknowledge that our past is holding us back.**
- **Being stuck in the past can make you angry, frustrated, resentful, and unable to enjoy the present.**
- **Comparing your past to your life today will only make you feel dissatisfied and stop you from having the motivation to move on.**
- **The process of moving on eventually leads to acceptance.**
- **Letting go takes time but you can do it!**

❦ 2 ❦
THE ART OF FORGIVENESS

"True forgiveness is when you can say 'Thank you for that experience'." –Oprah Winfrey

Forgiveness is a tough concept to practice when you feel you have been wronged. I absolutely get that and know most people find it extremely difficult to forgive anyone who has hurt them.

You may have been the victim of some terrible act or been caught up as an innocent bystander in a traumatic event. Forgiving the person or people who caused you or your loved ones emotional or physical harm can seem unthinkable.

Your memories also cause you to relive certain moments in the past that are still having a lasting effect on you today. Whatever happened to you must have been dreadful and I am not going to attempt to tell you otherwise.

At the same time, a lot of our memories can be quite unreliable - things said or done may not have played out exactly as we remember them in reality. Just in the same way that five witnesses to a traffic accident may all describe the event from a slightly different perspective, our perception of the past may not be completely watertight. A lot depends on the situation, our personality, how we were feeling at the time, and so many other factors.

The point is that often it is the emotion we are responding to that we felt at the time, and not the actual details of the occurrence.

But let's take a look at the art of forgiveness first and find out why being able to forgive is so empowering. The definition of forgiveness is to give up resentment for someone. It is a personal choice that we will often be confronted with in our lives and we won't always be able to forgive.

If you feel unable to totally forgive someone for any wrongdoing, how do you think this is affecting your life today?

Resentment, like all negative emotions, can have serious implications for our physical, emotional, and even spiritual health. If we suffer from long periods of mood disorders, this can lead to mild or even severe depression and we already know how that can affect our health.

Depression has been linked to heart disease, a compromised immune system, problems in our relationships with others, and an inability to carry on a normal life. When you think about it like that, forgiveness seems like a better option, doesn't it?

Why should I forgive?

You might still be carrying negative emotions from the past in your present, even though whatever happened to you took place last week, last year, or decades ago. It seems incredible, but we often bear the weight of pain and suffering for a lifetime, long after the event. Imagine if a child carried with them every single thing that happened while growing up– every scraped knee, every fall off a bike, every loss in a game, every harsh word by a parent or teacher.

Thankfully, most of us don't grow up with a long list of grudges starting from when we were five years old. And yet, we do tend to hold on to negative emotions for much longer than we should. Anger and resentment are two of them. In reality, forgiveness has many positive benefits for our mental and physical well-being.

- It stops us from licking old wounds that can never heal and allows us to find joy in our present-day lives.
- It releases us from being tied to the past and frees us to look forward to a brighter future.
- It brings us to a place of acceptance and inner peace.

One thing I want to point out is that pain is part of life. There will always be times when we feel hurt, disappointed, and even mistreated. I am not here to promise you that you will never be hurt again by someone or something.

But what I can tell you is that suffering is optional – it is in your hands to decide how long you are prepared to suffer for. Being unable to forgive is like prolonging that suffering because it keeps you in a mindset of pain and anger.

A study by Stanford University in 2003 looked at the process of forgiveness and came up with some interesting results[1]. Not much research had been done on the topic until then so the study began with the following assumptions:

1. The process of forgiveness remains the same, regardless of the incident.
2. Forgiveness has more to do with our past than our present life.
3. Forgiveness should be about all grievances, whether they are big or small.

The study showed that those people who learn to forgive can also:

- improve their psychological and physiological wellness
- make them emotionally stronger
- have greater confidence
- be more optimistic
- feel less stressed
- improve their overall health
- increase their positive emotions
- enjoy a happier outlook on life

Forgiveness can be practiced at all levels of pain, from someone being rude to you in the street to finding out your partner has been cheating on you. As the Dalai Lama has been quoted as saying, *"If I develop bad feelings toward those who make me suffer, this will only destroy my own peace of mind. But if I forgive, my mind becomes calm."*

Whatever age you are, you can benefit from learning how to forgive. You may have been raised in a neglectful family or experienced a lack of care when older. You might have been abused or had a partner who was unfaithful. All of these are examples of situations in which someone else inflicted pain on you, but holding on to that pain will prevent you from leading a happy, healthy life.

How can I learn to forgive?

The process of learning to forgive is not an easy one, and definitely not something you can achieve overnight. At the same time, when you are able to forgive, it can transform your life. It involves certain skills that you can learn, including acceptance, shifting perspectives, emotional regulation, compassion, and radical responsibility.

If that all sounds a bit too much for you to handle, there is no need to worry. Take each day as it comes and bear in mind why you are choosing to forgive. Let's be clear here – it is a choice that only you can make when you are ready and understand how it can benefit you.

You can start off by imagining how much more satisfied you will feel in your life, released from those shackles that someone else has placed on you with their actions. You hold the key to gaining your freedom.

1. Acceptance

You may think that acceptance is about defeat or resignation. You may even consider it to be a weakness. In reality, acceptance gives you the power to say, "Ok, this happened to me, and I'm moving on.' That takes a lot of strength and conviction, and you are capable of achieving it.

Once you achieve acceptance, you shift the balance, separating the pain of what happened from your tendency to keep suffering. It doesn't mean you liked what happened in the past or are happy that it did, but it does mean that you recognize it occurred and can't be undone.

2. Emotional regulation

If you can learn to regulate your emotions, your mind will follow suit. Rather than letting your flight or fight response kick in, you can work through those negative responses and filter out what you don't need. By all means, allow those negative emotions to arise, then put a label on them and regulate your response to them.

Let's say, for example, you experience stress when you recall painful memories. You feel tense, your hands become clammy, your throat tightens, and your heart begins to race. Notice those reactions and acknowledge them by saying to yourself: 'I feel stressed, I feel scared. I feel nervous, my heart is racing.'

Once you identify your emotions, you are allowing space for them to come to the surface. It's then easier to see what they are: grief, anger, and pain. All of these can arise when you think about someone who harmed you in the past but identifying them actually disempowers them. You can detach yourself from negative feelings and find some inner calm where your pain eventually lessens.

3. Shifting your perspectives

When you change your perspective, you can observe your thoughts, feelings, and bodily sensations from a different angle. Being aware of such sensations is different from experiencing them. Observing anger, for example, is not the same as being angry.

As soon as I start to feel upset about something, I press a pause button and stop to look at whatever emotion has come to the fore: anger, indignation, pain...whatever it may be. In that moment, I am focusing on the emotion as something detached from me and this helps me to see it for what it is.

I can then regain my inner balance very quickly and the negativity within me eventually passes. That doesn't mean I bury my emotions but quite the opposite. I have simply learned this technique of looking at them as an observer, rather than a participant. It's something you can try and, with practice, you will be able to shift your perspective and realize that your experiences don't define you.

4. Empathy and compassion

There is a lot to be said for empathy and compassion. Both of these skills allow you to understand what the other person is experiencing and can be stepping stones toward forgiveness. Empathy gives you insights into the pain of another and compassion can prompt you to take action to help reduce their pain.

This doesn't mean that you approve of their actions if they have wronged you. What it can help to do, though, is reach a level of acceptance for what they are experiencing, which can be liberating for you.

5. Accountability

This is when you can accept responsibility for yourself and own your actions, feelings, thoughts, and behavior. Reacting through fear or denying you have any power over how you feel will not help you to overcome bad experiences. You are, in effect, relinquishing your power over your life to someone else. It is your responsibility to take action to avoid behaving negatively as that hurts you in the end.

Tools for forgiveness

When you feel hurt, that feeling can grow like a tumor inside you. The more you feed it, the bigger it becomes. For forgiveness to come into your life, you must begin by taking responsibility for how you feel.

Yes, someone did something terrible to you, but are you prepared to let them keep hurting you long after the event? I am sure your answer will be, 'no', which is why you need to address your emotions now. That is not to say that you must like what has happened, and it is certainly not the case that what took place was your fault.

I want you to try my three tools for learning how to develop positive feelings and disarm the negative ones that are holding you back in life.

One – Select your responses

If you focus too much on what is wrong with your life, how about diverting your attention to the things you can be grateful for? You wouldn't select a TV channel that shows programs you don't like, so why choose that option in real life? You would select the one that entertains, amuses, and gives you pleasure, right?

Learn to change channels when something offends you or annoys you, such as someone being rude to you in a store. Instead of letting their comments ruin your day, how about reminding yourself what a beautiful day it is or recalling the thrill of seeing your newborn baby for the first time?

Here are some examples of how to switch from negative to positive in your daily life:

- At a restaurant, be thankful for the tasty food and focus less on the bad service.
- At work, appreciate your great colleagues and focus less on your boss's bad attitude.
- When you are stuck in traffic, listen to your favorite music and forget about the congestion.
- Take a walk in nature and marvel at its beauty rather than complain about the city's smog.
- Visit a gallery or museum and admire the exhibition instead of worrying about your financial woes.
- Respond to smiles from strangers and don't dwell on rude people you might meet.
- Be joyful about the simple things in life and let your mind rest.

Two – Practice breathwork

Breathing is something we do without thinking, but breathwork involves concentrating on your breath to help focus your mind and soul. All you need to do is allocate a few minutes each day wherever you are to get the most out of this kind of exercise.

- Stop what you are doing, sit down, and focus on your breathing.

- Notice each breath you inhale and exhale, feeling the sensation as you do so.
- Inhale and exhale slowly, bringing your mind to your breath and nothing else.
- Do this 4-5 times and on each inhale, silently say 'thank you' as you embrace how fortunate you are.
- Do this for 4-5 more times, with full focus on your breath as you repeat each 'thank you'..
- Allow yourself to breathe normally when done and get back to what you were doing.

Three – Find your heart

This is a very therapeutic way of reconnecting with feelings of love, peace, and contentment. All you need to do is practice a few times a week and you will notice the difference.

- Begin by drawing attention to your breathing
- Conjure up in your mind moments when you felt serene or blissful. This could have been when you were with loved ones, or while sitting in a park or on a beach.
- Recall those feelings of love, warmth, and happiness and enjoy them.
- If you lose your attention, gently bring it back to those feelings.
- Try to sit in this tranquil state for about 15 minutes.

Learning to forgive won't necessarily take all of the pain away from what you endured, but it can help you to live your present life with more happiness. While holding on to those intense emotions of anger, grief, and sadness can seem natural to you, the truth is that they are harming you. Once you begin to let go, each new day will seem more wonderful than the last.

Making memories

Every time you recall a new memory, not only are you reinforcing it but you are also embellishing it. Memories fade and we often construct new ones with new details of what actually happened. The story that we tell ourselves changes each time it is repeated for various reasons.

We may recall what we believe to be true about the past, or wish were true. Depending on who we are talking to about it, we may omit some details or add others. This creates a new narrative of events each time you tell it.

When we describe our memories to different audiences, we also change the memory, and this is something known as the *audience-tuning effect*. We aren't deliberately trying to deceive anyone or lie when this happens. It is just our way of making the story 'work' for the intended audience.

If you keep adding or taking away from your story – your memory of an event – it is quite likely that the present story differs greatly from the original one. That's not to say that something bad never happened to you, but your 'current version' of it may be slightly skewed. And you are probably giving it way more attention than it now deserves.

For example, you might have the same basic memories as your siblings about your days growing up together, while each one of you will give a slightly different version about the day the dog got lost, or the time when your house was flooded. Neither of you is wrong when telling your version of events, but you will notice that there are several discrepancies.

With our memories being so unreliable, it makes you wonder why we hold onto them as if they were the gospel truth. More often than not, they are amended versions of what happened to us in the past.

Moving on and trying to forgive doesn't mean you will forget what happened to you. What it *does* mean is that you can lead a more content life and embrace the wonderful person you are today, despite your painful past. Then, you will eventually be ready to fully let go and be free.

Key highlights

- **Learning to forgive can liberate you from past pain**

- **Forgiveness brings joy into our lives and inner peace.**
- **People who learn to forgive also improve their psychological and physiological wellness, feel less stressed, and more optimistic about the future**
- **Acceptance, emotional regulation, and empathy are just some of the ways to practice forgiveness**
- **Being selective, practicing breathwork, and recalling moments of joy are useful tools to achieve forgiveness.**
- **Our memories aren't always reliable and rumination can lead to increased mental health problems, unhealthy coping skills, and constant negative thinking.**

3
DEALING WITH PAINFUL MEMORIES

'Forget what hurt you in the past. But never forget what it taught you.' –
Anonymous

We are slaves to our past in many ways. We continue to wear the shackles that keep us there by bringing up old memories time and time again.

Whatever you went through that caused hurt, reminding yourself of it every day is only going to keep hurting you. This is why it is essential to leave some aspects of your past behind. How can you do that, you may ask, if you have no control over what memories come into your mind?

What if I tell you that it is possible to deal with those painful memories when they spring up, even if you cannot control when they choose to appear? That's right: you can learn to take away their hold over you and not be weighed down by pain time after time.

This also applies to less serious events that you keep going over in your mind, such as being told off by your boss the other day or having an argument with a best friend. You might replay conversations over and over in your mind where spiteful things were said or keep replaying the events of your last bad date.

While it is OK to work out what went wrong and the lessons to be learned from past experiences, rumination (repetitive negative thought process) can be harmful. The longer you dwell on your problems, the more you magnify your misfortune, which eventually causes you even more distress.

Recalling bad memories can be very unhealthy for us. Each time we go over old traumas, it affects our well-being and can lead to:

- **Unhealthy coping skills.** When you ruminate, chewing over those bad memories constantly, this causes emotional distress. When that happens, you might be more likely to find unhealthy ways of coping, such as resorting to alcohol or drugs.
- **Permanent negative thinking**. Negative thinking can become a bad habit that makes it difficult to think positively and enjoy life, even when your circumstances are healthy and stable.

Why do my bad memories haunt me?

Research from 2021[1] suggests that we are more likely to remember a stressful event than an insignificant one and this is due to our neurobiology. When you are in an emotionally charged situation, more areas of the brain become active. Even when the experience is in the past, your nervous system can still react as if it is going through the same situation.

That's because every time you relive a memory, your brain recalls the reactions you had back then and reproduces them as if the event is happening now.

Think of a time when you faced extreme danger, and try to recall the sensations you felt then.

Did your heart rate increase?

Did your muscles tense up?

Did you feel like you were preparing for a life-death struggle?

Did you begin to perspire profusely? (This helps to cool you down and improve the ability to grip for extra traction if you need to escape)

Did you freeze and feel unable to move?

Did your senses become more acute?

Did your hearing amplify?

Did you feel tingling or numbness in your limbs?

Did you experience shortness of breath?

Did you feel dizzy or think you were going to faint?

Did your mind go blank or was it racing?

Did you feel a sense of helplessness, terror, panic, or chaos?

These are all physiological responses activated by your brain that we humans have developed throughout our evolution. They are automatic and cannot be stopped once initiated, as our brain goes into survival mode. And they can be reactivated even when you aren't in danger.

The amygdala, which I mentioned earlier, is located deep within the medial temporal lobe and it is a bit like air traffic control. Its job is to process any sensory threats and send instructions to other parts of the brain, like the hypothalamus, which releases stress hormones.

The brain stem areas are also notified and these control the levels of alertness and automatic behaviors in the limbic system.

We might be unconsciously responding to threats, in which the amygdala fires off a rapid, but imprecise response. Conscious responses of which we are aware are channeled through the cortical sensory areas to provoke more complex responses by the amygdala.

This explains how our brain responds to threats even before we are consciously aware of them. For example, if you are sitting alone at night and hear a sudden noise, your amygdala immediately sets off a rapid response, making you freeze for a moment. On the other hand, if you see a bear running toward you while walking in the forest, you consciously begin to plan your escape route.

How does all of this fit into the subject of memories? Well, traumatic memories especially are intensely powerful. When people talk about memories, they are usually referring to conscious or explicit memories. However, the brain can actually encode both explicit and implicit memories in parallel for the same event.

The threat response

Implicit memory can be threat conditioning, which means that every time you recall it, you respond in exactly the same way as when it originally happened to you. In laboratory experiments, when a harmful stimulus such as an electric shock is paired with a certain image or sound, the brain forms an association between the neutral stimulus and the threat response.

After that, anyone who took part in the experiment that is exposed to this image or sound will react as if they are also exposed to the electric shock. These threat responses can last for life and are one way we have managed to survive so long as a species. On the downside, we often respond to threats brought on by memories, even when the reality is that we are completely safe.

If you have ever been in a car accident, the sight of a vehicle approaching you that resembles the one you collided with years ago can cause you to sweat as your heart rate increases. These responses are activated even if they don't come with conscious recollections of trauma.

What we do know is that those traumatic memories are less organized than memories acquired under less stressful conditions but they are extremely vivid and intense. They also happen to be more persistent, which is why they keep coming back to haunt you over and over again.

When you keep going over those painful memories, you're literally being kept in a state of hypervigilance or emotional distress. That is why it is important to deal with these feelings as they arise and to create space for your emotions attached to those memories to surface.

If you are experiencing severe flashbacks of events, you might be suffering from PTSD, in which case, you should seek the help and support of a trained mental health professional.

Remodifying memories

Here's the interesting thing: as you read in the previous chapter, memories aren't all that reliable. In fact, although our brains are pretty good at recording bad memories, they aren't immediately saved in the hard drive and can be modified and transformed.

Studies show that we have a two to three hours window before the memory is filed in our long-term memory after sitting in the short-term memory for a while. It's one of the reasons why many therapists ask patients to recall their traumatic memories, albeit in a safe space, to allow for a kind of 'remodification' or healing.

Imagine, for example, that you get bitten by a dog while out walking one day. If this memory is left to bury itself deep within your long-term memory as a traumatic experience, it will resurface as one in the future. Of course, it is a terrible thing to happen and may cause you physical as well as psychological harm. But if you can process it just after the event you might be able to put it into some kind of perspective.

The dog was scared or triggered by something you did. It was acting on instinct and doesn't use logic like we humans do. It might have bitten into your skin, but the damage isn't too serious. I'm not saying you should dismiss it, but working through what happened as soon as possible can help you to disconnect the memory from later 'alarm' mechanisms that can occur in the future.

If you don't deal with the event after it happens, you may develop a fear of dogs for many years to come, have panic attacks when you come close to one, and even experience stress when thinking about the event. You might have heard people say, 'When you fall off a horse, get straight back on'.

It seems to make sense in this context because if you do have such an unfortunate accident and don't resaddle, you could walk away with a lifetime fear of horse riding after that.

We need to heal after a traumatic experience in our past, although it is often buried and not dealt with. This is especially true if you suffered something unpleasant as a child. As an adult, you are much better equipped to deal with negative experiences as they occur and neuroscience is on your side.

A simple, yet effective, method for dealing with bad past experiences is to rewire the brain and convert negative emotions to positive ones. Neuropsychologists like Rick Hanson talk about these kinds of techniques[2] and offer us a way to heal after trying to come to terms with past events. There are four steps to this technique:

Step 1: Have a positive experience. As a negative memory comes into your mind, draw on a positive experience and bring it into your awareness. In the case of being bitten by a dog, whenever you remember the incident, tune into any other experience where you felt safe and supported.

Step 2: Enrich it. Rather than ruminating for days over a bad experience, take time to deepen that positive experience you are drawing on. Create an image of someone you feel happy with or a place where you feel content and loved. Keep recalling this image in mind every time you realize the bad memory is popping up.

Step 3: Absorb it. Imagine that you are breathing in the positive experience, allowing it to reach every cell of your body. Allow it to be fully absorbed, fusing with your mind, heart, and soul.

Step 4: Link positive and negative material. If you feel able to, you can begin to link the negative experience with the more positive one. Imagine, for example, that you are served a delicious dinner, where you begin to pick out the ingredients that you aren't too keen on. You can still enjoy the dinner because you are in control of what you do or do not eat. By letting go of the negatives, you can gradually reduce their impact on you.

It is possible to stop dwelling on painful memories when they arise and rewire your brain to get out of that negative loop. Some of the most effective ways to do that are:

Recognize what's happening. The more you ruminate, the more you will get stuck in a mindset of negative thinking. From now on, try to be more aware of what brings on these memories - what causes them to appear in your mind? As soon as you spot them, replace them with something more pleasant that happened to you recently.

Find solutions. Did you know that thinking about what happened in the past isn't helping you in the present? At the same time, finding ways to resolve this is essential.

It goes back to that old adage of learning from your mistakes. If, for example, you were attacked while out one night, think of ways you can prevent that from happening again, such as restricting your movements after dark, never going out alone, and so on.

Distract yourself. When you are busy doing nothing, old memories seem to find a way to enter your mind. Although it is important to process any buried emotions, going over the same old story will drain you and leave you emotionally exhausted. Instead, distract yourself with an activity every time you find yourself ruminating and use your time productively rather than wallowing in the painful past.

Distance yourself. That could be physical distance from the person or situation who hurt you or psychological distance between yourself and the negative experience.

When you can achieve that, your brain doesn't have to have to think about it, process it, or be reminded of it. You can do this by:

Having a 'letting go' ceremony

Removing old photos that bring back specific memories

Removing any objects from your space that remind you of the past, such as clothes or ornaments

Emotional responses

When we recall negative memories, we can also feel all kinds of emotions, ranging from anger or sadness to embarrassment or disappointment. I want you to think of something that happened to you in the recent past that wasn't too traumatic - maybe having to speak in front of a room of people, or being late for an important appointment.

How did you feel then? Do you sense the same emotions rising within you now? You may do, and this is because the incident impacted you negatively at the time.

Just thinking about it may even make you feel like you weren't good enough, or didn't live up to your own expectations, and these thoughts can affect your actions. When you felt embarrassed about being late, recalling this may make you less inclined to make commitments in the future for fear of experiencing negative emotions again.

Cognitive responses

A real traumatic event in your past is a major event that can continue to impact your life today, affecting your mental health. Victims of abuse find it very hard to trust others and will feel threatened by any kind of behavior that triggers those memories.

As a result, many victims of abuse are more at risk of suffering from health problems such as anxiety, depression, and high levels of stress. Someone who is abused as a child may be hesitant to trust others or feel threatened by behavior that triggers memories of past abuse well into adulthood.

Physical responses

Returning to the dog bite scenario, you may be afraid to go back to the same location because of the painful memories associated with it. If you do go back, you might notice your heart rate go up, your breathing becomes more shallow, and even begin to shake.

You can also experience all of these sensations just by recalling the memory of what happened. The stress can eventually lead to problems with our health, such as gastrointestinal, musculoskeletal, and respiratory issues[3].

It's definitely not easy to stop painful memories from coming to mind, but there are ways you can deal with the emotions they invoke. By reframing the negative memories and focusing on positive aspects, as I mentioned earlier, it is possible to manage your emotions.

Rather than trying to suppress what you went through, reflecting on it accompanied by positive elements can really help.

More tips to help you move on

There is more than one way to move on from painful memories. Below you will find some ideas and as you read them, you can consider which one(s) that best complement your existing situation and lifestyle.

1. Avoid people or places that might trigger negative reactions
2. Incorporate some self-care into your daily routine
3. Spend more time with positive people who can offer you support
4. Silence negative thoughts and turn up the volume on positive self-talk
5. Don't ignore your emotions, but simply observe them
6. Get off social media for a while and enjoy real life
7. Accept that you may never receive an apology from your wrongdoer
8. Forgive yourself for things you have done in the past that you now regret
9. Write down new goals or dreams for your future
10. Give gratitude each morning or last thing at night for all the good things in your life

While bad memories play out in our heads, they can also affect our relationships because of the way they make us feel. It's very important to be able to talk about what you are going through with someone you trust. It could be a family member, a friend, or a health professional and as long as you are open to that, you can begin to feel less isolated and hopeless.

Reach out to someone and help yourself to heal from your past – you have a wonderful future waiting for you just around the corner!

Key highlights

- **Constantly recalling old traumas can lead to increased mental health problems, unhealthy coping skills, and negative thinking.**
- **We are more likely to remember a stressful event because of our neurobiology.**
- **Traumatic memories are threat responses that can last a lifetime if we don't deal with them.**
- **Memories can be remodified in the brain before being stored in its long-term memory.**
- **It is possible to convert negative memories to positive ones.**
- **Negative memories affect us physically, emotionally, and psychologically.**

❧ 4 ☙
THE MIND-BODY DYNAMIC

'Being traumatized is not just an issue of being stuck in the past; it is just as much a problem of not being fully alive in the present.' —Bessel A. van der Kolk

We used to think that our minds were completely separate from our bodies, thanks to a long line of philosophical thought that dominated western history. It was assumed that our thoughts don't affect us physically because there was no connection between the mental and the physical.

Now we know that isn't true. When you have continuous negative thoughts, keep ruminating over past events, and your present life is disrupted by your mental state, these experiences have an impact on your body. We already read in the last chapter about how our brain controls our physical responses when we relive painful memories and the body does indeed store those memories.

A traumatic experience can stay in the body, later showing itself in physical symptoms like headaches, chronic pain, and disassociation. Your brain might already 'be over' the negative experience, but your body still remembers it, even if you are unaware of it.

Trauma expert Bessel van der Kolk talked at length about this in his well-known book The Body Keeps the Score[1], and a lot of research has been done recently on the subject.

About half of Americans will go through at least one traumatic event in their lives. Those survivors of trauma are three times more likely to suffer from irritable bowel syndrome, chronic pain, fibromyalgia, and chronic fatigue syndrome.

Trauma has also been linked to type 2 diabetes, heart disease, and rheumatoid arthritis. Having said that, undergoing a traumatic experience doesn't necessarily mean that you will suffer some kind of health problem later. Other things do come into play, such as your life experiences, support from loved ones, and your genes.

With the right support, it is possible to heal from trauma. Methods used by healthcare professionals include things like cognitive processing therapy (CPT), prolonged exposure (PE) therapy, and Eye Movement Desensitization and Reprocessing (EMDR) therapy. All are very useful in processing trauma that is held in the body.

What is trauma?

According to the Substance Abuse and Mental Health Services Administration (SAMSHA), trauma is defined as any emotional or physical response to one or more harmful or life-threatening events or circumstances with lasting adverse effects on your mental and physical well-being,

It seems incredible to think that something that happened to us in our childhood, or even in our recent past, can continue to severely affect our well-being in the present. It is also a real pity if this applies to you because until you find strategies to deal with that, you will always be stuck in the past. No one wants to be held back from enjoying life in the here and now, and I am sure you are not even aware of what is happening to you.

To start understanding how you feel, I want to ask you how many of the symptoms below you experience regularly:

- feeling easily overwhelmed
- feeling 'on edge'
- muscle tension
- chest tightness
- trouble sleeping
- nightmares
- memory issues
- brain fog or trouble focusing
- anxiety and avoidance
- depression
- Dissociation
- Chronic pain
- Headaches

These are all signs that your nervous system is on 'high alert', always ready to deal with the next threat, even when no threat really exists.

One of my good friends, Sarah, is a prime example of this. She grew up in foster care and was often neglected and psychologically abused by her 'carers.' When she was 18, she left home and began to make her own way, finally meeting her husband Ross a few years later. Although happily married, she began having panic attacks for no apparent reason.

She also began having terrible pains in her legs although her medical doctor couldn't find any obvious physiological cause for that. She was referred to a psychologist who probed into Sarah's past and learned of her traumatic upbringing.

Sarah had never told anyone before about her awful childhood and had even tried to erase it from her own memory. But those memories were still there.

It's not that trauma was physically sitting somewhere in her muscles or bones, but in those memory and emotional centers of her hippocampus and amygdala. These put the body on high alert whenever something reminds them of the past traumatic event.

If you have suffered any kind of trauma that has not been resolved, you will also have less tolerance for stress. Sarah, for example, felt completely overwhelmed whenever a row brewed up between herself and her husband and would begin to shake, teeth chattering, and hands going clammy.

Ross was a great guy and rows between couples are common, but Sarah's flight or fight mechanism would be automatically activated. She was unable to handle any kind of confrontation in a calm, logical manner as her brain's threat responses took over.

When you keep reliving the experience of the past through memories, it reinforces this threat response even more and definitely needs to be addressed. When we leave things buried, our brain continues to increase the levels of stress hormones in our bodies, which can make us feel 'on edge' a lot of the time.

Many people resort to mood-altering substances to 'deal' with their emotions and psychological discomfort, which can lead to addiction and other harmful kinds of behavior.

This constant state of hypervigilance might not make any sense because you are safe, but the body thinks otherwise. As it is your brain that is in charge of rational thought, it can be very difficult to snap out of this kind of response. The part of the brain responsible for executive functioning shuts down when your amygdala is on high alert, making it difficult to stay grounded and present in a meaningful way.

So, how can you help yourself to overcome these physical reactions to a past trauma? If you feel unable to cope, I would advise you to seek out professional help. In the meantime, here are some strategies that you can introduce into your daily life to help you on your healing journey.

Non-judgment

When you feel those physical responses arising in response to an imagined threat, try not to judge your reaction. Your body has been programmed to respond in this way and it is not something to be ashamed of. Rather than experiencing self-loathing because of your inability to cope, acknowledge that these reactions are occurring for a reason.

Say to yourself, 'My reaction is legitimate and nothing to be ashamed of' when you notice them arise. Acknowledge them without criticizing yourself for being this way.

Permission

You have every right to feel the way you do and can give yourself permission to do so. If you feel numb, it could be because you believe you are not allowed to feel certain emotions.

Maybe you think you are not supposed to cry or get angry and try to suppress those emotions. The truth is that all emotions are legitimate and, as humans, we naturally experience a wide range of them so denying yourself certain feelings will not make you feel any better.

Say to yourself, 'I allow myself to feel this way' when anger or pain begin to arise within you. As you allow those feelings to come to the fore, you are creating space for healing.

Release

Now that you've given yourself permission to feel without judgment, you can begin to release that emotion from your body. Just as a dog shakes to rid itself of stress, you can begin shaking your own body. Begin by wiggling your feet, then your arms, and your head.

Sing or dance if you feel like it, and get rid of those pent-up emotions that you do not need anymore. You may even begin to cry, and that is a great natural way for your body to release stress so don't try to fight it.

Say to yourself, 'I am releasing all of my negative emotions,' and as you do so, you will begin to feel relieved and less tense.

If this kind of approach doesn't appeal to you, that is fine. You may want to grab a notebook and write down everything you are feeling. Once you are done, you can tear it into tiny shreds and bin it - those emotions are now released from your mind and body.

Forgiveness

Here, I am talking about forgiving yourself, which is crucial if you want to move on in your life. 'Forgiveness for what?' you may ask. How about forgiveness for thinking you were to blame for something that happened to you? Perhaps you need self-forgiveness for something terrible you did in the past that haunts you.

It could be that you need to ask yourself for forgiveness for not being the father, mother, daughter, son, or friend you should have been. Your emotions may keep reminding you of your past pain but once you can forgive yourself, you remove the hold that they have over you.

Say to yourself,' I forgive myself because I did the best I could at the time and I am willing to learn from my mistakes.'

Move on knowing that you have the knowledge and tools to think differently next time.

Time

They say that time is a healer but this isn't the case if you leave open wounds unattended. All they do over time is continue to ooze and fill you with toxicity. Time can heal but only when you have tended to those wounds and given them your care.

You could often find yourself relapsing into old patterns and behaviors and when you do so, be kind to yourself. It might take years before you can reach full non-judgment, forgiveness, and release but if you keep at it, you will get there eventually.

An action plan to overcome past emotions trapped inside your body

Trying to work through any past trauma can be overwhelming and may be too intense for you at this moment. You can ease into overcoming those past emotions if you begin to incorporate an action plan into your life. Here are my tips to do just that:

Move your body

Try to exercise for 30 minutes or more each day. There is nothing better to get rid of stress and restore your body's natural equilibrium.

Run, walk, swim, dance – and as you do, focus on your body and not on your problems.

Add a mindfulness element. Instead of focusing on your thoughts or distracting yourself while you exercise, really focus on your body and how it feels, not your thoughts. Notice the sensation of the blood pumping around your torso and limbs and feel the sweat on your skin. Enjoy those sensations of being alive and full of positive energy.

Be sociable

Staying locked in your own thoughts is like creating your own dungeon. It can be dark, and very lonely. That is why you need to connect more with other people, especially those who can help you heal. You might feel the urge to withdraw but that can only make you feel worse.

You don't have to share your painful memories with everyone and it is actually a good idea to talk about something else to take your mind off things.

Spend time with friends, and engage in social activities (preferably face-to-face and not online). Do stuff with other people, such as going shopping or watching a soccer game, and put your traumatic experiences away for the time being.

Reach out

If you want to talk to someone about what you went through, join a support group and connect with others who are facing the same problems as yourself. This is a great way to be inspired as you work toward overcoming any issues and you will not feel alone anymore.

You can even volunteer to do charity work or help out with a local organization. By volunteering, you will feel more empowered and realize you have many strengths that can be of use to others less fortunate than you.

Make new friends

Friends can give invaluable support when you need it and if you find yourself without friends, now is the time to make some new ones. You might find this hard to do, but if you read my book **How To Make Friends Easily**, you will find plenty of practical tips on how to get out there and meet new people. It's easy to think that no one will understand you; that no one has been through what you did, but you will be surprised. Everyone has a story to tell and even if it isn't the same as yours, you will find a lot of people going through some struggle of their own who would be only too happy to share it with you.

Self-regulate

When you learn to self-regulate your nervous system, you reclaim control of your reactions to stress and anxiety. If you begin to feel disoriented, upset, or dizzy, for example, focus on your breathing.

This is a brilliant way to calm yourself and it only takes a few moments. Breathe in and out for 60 seconds while concentrating on your breath and nothing else. Once you get used to doing this, you will soon see how quickly you come down to a calm, stable state.

Look after your health

I know you have heard it many times before, but having a healthy body will increase your ability to cope with stress. By eating healthily and having plenty of exercise, your immune system will be in tip-top shape and more able to fight off stress-related illnesses.

Apart from that, you will simply feel great. Having enough relaxation time is just as important as a good night's sleep and you should establish a daily routine of work, rest, and sleep.

Be sure to relax

Relaxation techniques you can try include yoga, meditation, or mindfulness exercises that you do at a set time each day. Playing a sport or being engaged in your favorite hobby or pastime are also wonderful ways to look after your physical, mental, and psychological health.

Growing from trauma

Studies have shown that survivors of trauma can heal and even grow into stronger, more driven, more resilient individuals. Resilience is the ability to handle any problematic situations more effectively with less stress and emotional fallout. Post Traumatic Growth is a method some therapists use that can help you heal from your traumatic past and become more driven.

You can begin this process of change by looking at the positives of anything from your past and embracing optimism about your future. It's not about undermining what happened to you but offering a way for you to move on from that.

When you consider the strengths you have used to cope with your past trauma, you will also identify new strengths that will also equip you to deal with any future challenges.

1. Start by listing five personal strengths that you already had before your painful experience.
2. Next, identify which of those strengths helped you to deal with the trauma.
3. Now list any new strengths you feel you've developed as a result. What are these new strengths?
4. What are your thoughts and feelings about these new personal strengths?

When you become aware of what you have overcome, and the new strengths you have gained as a result of that, it can make you feel more balanced and positive. These are useful tools to add to your tool kit when difficulties arise again. You are a survivor and should be very proud of yourself!

You may find that you have developed new strengths in many aspects of your life and should embrace these changes. For example,

- You can relate more easily to others
- You are more able to express your emotions
- You have more compassion for others
- You have developed new interests
- You are more likely to change things you don't like
- You have a greater feeling of self-reliance.

- You are better able to accept outcomes.
- You feel more in tune with your spiritual side
- You appreciate your life more

I hope you feel inspired to believe in the vast potential you have to grow and be happy. No one deserves to suffer and I believe we can all overcome that by taking steps to heal from trauma and become a more purpose-driven person.

While your mind and body may act in unison, you are the boss and should never forget that!

Key highlights

- **Trauma is any emotional or physical response to one or more harmful or life-threatening event or circumstances.**
- **Traumatic experiences can have lasting adverse effects on your mental and physical well-being,**
- **These experiences can stay in the body and later show themselves in physical symptoms like chronic pain and illnesses.**
- **With the right support, it is possible to heal from trauma.**
- **Strategies to self-heal include non-judgment, forgiveness, and release.**
- **Practical everyday activities to overcome past traumas include being active, spending time with friends, healthy eating, and volunteering.**
- **Post Traumatic Growth comes from looking at the positives of anything from your past and embracing optimism about your future.**

5
THE TRIGGER IS THE GUN

'The people who trigger us to feel negative emotions are messengers. They are messengers for the unhealed parts of our being.' –Teal Swan

One day, I was driving to my office and listening to my favorite radio station. Suddenly, I felt overcome by a terrible sadness and tears began to stream down my face without warning. It was the song that was playing—some sentimental love song–that took me back to the moment when my old boyfriend told me we were through almost 15 years ago.

Although I am happily married and never think about that guy at all, the song triggered something deep inside of me. It was the pain of rejection and it still hurt.

Emotional triggers can do that to us. One minute we feel fine and the next, a sound, a person, an event, an image, or any other kind of experience can cause us to have an emotional reaction.

How many times have you felt yourself being triggered by something, leading you to have a change of mood? We are all triggered by certain things into having an emotional response and not all of those triggers are negative.

Sometimes, we can be stimulated to feel joy or be reminded of happy memories, such as when we see a photo that reminds us of a wonderful holiday we had. Despite that, 'being triggered' has come to be used as a term to describe a negative feeling – one that makes us feel sad, angry, hurt, ashamed, and so on.

I believe that these kinds of triggers aren't necessarily a bad thing as they may be exposing some unresolved issues that we still haven't dealt with. For example, in my case, that fear of rejection resurfaced when I heard the song playing in my car. It wasn't about the person who rejected me. It was more to do with the pain I felt at the time, which affected my self-esteem for quite a while after that. Even now, I admit that I don't take rejection too well but it is something I am aware of and constantly working on.

From a mental health perspective, the term 'trigger' refers to any situation that acts as a catalyst for some kind of emotional, physical, or behavioral response. Once triggered, the person might have a severe reaction and experience an increase in unpleasant emotions.

Triggers usually happen before we are even aware of them, sending our bodies into survival responses of fight, flight, or freeze. When we have a lot of bad memories or suffered some kind of trauma in the past, we may get triggered too often and that can interfere with our lives.

Old memories can cause us a lot of heartache in the present, causing emotional and physical reactions that we seem unable to control. But triggers can also lead us to a place of healing, showing us where we need to do more work to overcome our negative emotions. They are, in fact, a nudge toward self-reflection and self-awareness.

The thing with triggers is that our reactions can happen so fast that we don't notice the difference between the stimulus and the response.

This just leaves us feeling confused and overwhelmed. When we learn the skills to identify and handle our triggers, we can gain a better understanding of why we react the way we do, and master the art of handling that more effectively.

The more self-awareness we have, the more difficult it is for triggers to set us off on a rollercoaster of emotions that can affect our emotional well-being.

Recognizing your triggers

We all have different emotional triggers, most of which are unwanted and uncomfortable memories or experiences. Not all strong emotional responses are trigger reactions, though. For example, if you receive some news about a friend or relative being seriously ill, it is natural to feel distressed and worried. No one would expect you to avoid these emotions or try to control them. Triggers are different because they are like pinpricks, reminding you of something from your past that doesn't contribute to your well-being in the present.

We can put the categories of triggers into some general scenarios:

- Feeling self-conscious
- Being discounted
- Feeling we are being controlled
- Feeling taken advantage of
- Feeling vulnerable
- Experiences associated with relationships, such as loneliness or feeling suffocated
- Boundary concerns
- Feeling uncomfortable about what is happening
- Fearing what might happen

Within any of these categories, we may experience feelings of:

- Betrayal
- Rejection
- Insecurity
- Fear
- Anger
- Confusion
- Pain
- And more...

You might notice that every trigger on the list is part of life – all triggers are. We live, have relationships, and experience life events, so we are always going to go through a whole range of emotions and that is perfectly natural.

And yet, some of those experiences can be traumatic or painful and when we are reminded of them, that can be devastating. Sometimes those memories have been repressed and are silently waiting for us to address them. Other times, mad memories are constantly prodding us and demanding our attention.

Triggers can also have a physical effect on us, and being aware of that is a good start to dealing with them.

You might notice when you feel triggered that your heart begins to pound, your stomach churns, dizziness and uncontrollable shaking overtake you, and you break out into a cold sweat. That's your amygdala going into high alert and the sooner you recognize that, the easier it will be to calm yourself down.

I want to ask you three questions. You don't need to answer immediately but think of them as prompts to help you become more self-aware of your emotions. Here goes:

Do you know what your triggers are? Are they people, places, sounds, memories, or something else?

If you can identify your triggers, what personal issues do you feel they are directing you to?

Do you feel ready and able to deal with those issues?

It isn't easy to suddenly say, 'Oh, yes. I am triggered by a certain place and it makes me feel like this or that.' That's because of the stimulus-response equation I mentioned earlier. We often just don't realize we are being triggered and don't understand why we suddenly feel down, upset, or angry.

It is like one big knot that needs untying but I can assure you that with patience and determination, you will eventually be able to undo it.

Managing your triggers

The moment you feel physically or emotionally affected by something without any 'apparent' reason, stop to think if you are being triggered. Nine times out of ten, this will be the case. To help you respond to those emotions that seem to appear from nowhere, you first need to own them.

Feeling afraid, angry, or sad? It is OK to have those feelings because they are natural reactions to something you went through in the past. Anyone would feel the same in your position. Just by accepting that those emotions are there, you are on the way to learning to deal with them.

Let's imagine a friend commenting on your new haircut. An innocent thing like this may remind you of a time in the past when someone made fun of you for the way you looked. So, on this occasion, you react defensively and feel threatened.

- Just there, where you are going onto automatic pilot, catch yourself.
- Acknowledge how you are feeling.
- Recognize that a past event is causing you to feel this pain.
- Understand that this present incident is not a repeat of your past.
- Take back control and choose a different response.
- Give yourself some space if you need a few moments to calm down.
- Try to focus on your breathing and ground yourself in this present moment.

You aren't trying to avoid whatever triggered your emotions. You are just allowing yourself to acknowledge them and allow them to pass.

- **Expressing how you feel**

When someone close to you tends to trigger you often, opening up to them may help to avoid that happening in the future. If your partner keeps inadvertently opening up old wounds with their actions or comments, you really need to talk to them and communicate how you feel.

By using 'I' statements, which reflect how you feel without apportioning blame, you can explain what it is that is triggering you.

For instance, when your partner doesn't answer your text messages or calls, triggering a feeling of being disregarded, it is OK to say:

'I get angry when you don't reply to me. It feels like you don't care about me.'

When a close friend makes a joke about your driving abilities, touching a nerve, it's OK to say:

'I don't like it when you criticize me. It makes me feel worthless.'

- **Listing your triggers**

You can also name your triggers, or make a list of the ones you have identified. These could be tastes, sounds, locations, words, or behaviors. Knowing what they are helps you to spot them in good time so you can be prepared to tackle them.

And, it goes without saying that if you haven't found a way to deal with a particular trigger, it is best to avoid it. You don't need to go to a particular restaurant if it brings back bad memories, or hang out with a friend who reminds you of a traumatic experience.

- **Finding the source**

When you know what the source of your trigger reaction is, you will find it a lot easier to cope with it. Whatever happened in the past has a tendency to haunt our present but such events can also give us a window into who we really are all of our fears, insecurities, and doubts are exposed when we feel triggered and if you can dig deep enough to see what they are, you can process them much more effectively.

If, let's say, a particular world bothers you, such as 'stupid' or 'useless', why is that making you feel so bad? Who told you that you were stupid in the past: a teacher, carer, or partner? What does that tell you about your self-esteem at this moment? Is it possible that you need to work on that?

- **Watch out for projection**

Just because someone abused you physically or psychologically in the past, this doesn't mean that others will abuse you today. A loud voice doesn't always mean that someone is angry at you or about to assault you. Although your brain may think it does, loud voices and abuse are not inevitably linked. Can you make that distinction and not let that bad experience invade your present? Just because your ex left you for someone else, that doesn't mean you aren't attractive or unloveable.

Be careful when entering into new relationships so that you don't carry this false illusion with you. Your ex is one person – your new partner is someone completely different.

- **Noticing the signs**

As I said above, our body shows us signs that we are being triggered by putting us into a state of hyperarousal. As the cortisol and adrenaline pump through us, we may feel dizzy, disoriented, or nauseous.

If you cannot self-regulate in that moment, the first thing you need to do is calm yourself down. Get into the habit of having a favorite relaxation technique, such as focusing on your breath, going for a quick walk, or having a glass of water. Whatever brings your focus back to the present moment will allow the fight/flight response to subside.

- **Listening to your inner critic**

I know that I usually say ignore your inner voice, but in the case of being triggered, it is useful to listen to what it is really saying. The more you confront that, the sooner you will be able to get to the bottom of what is nagging at you.

Instead, once your negative self-talk begins to put you down, have a response ready, as if you were turning off an alarm clock. When your inner critic tells you, "I knew you were a failure,' respond to it with something like, 'I trust myself to do the best I can.' This is part of self-care, in which you can use your inner critic to prompt you to say something more positive about yourself.

- **Showing your emotions**

When we are triggered, we internalize all of those negative emotions, much like shaking a bottle of Champagne without removing the cork. It can feel very overwhelming if you don't have a vent for them.

Intense emotions like anger, sadness, and fear need to be released and it is OK to show them.

Being able to show your feelings might not be something you are used to, but you can at least vocalize them, which is one way of finding a release. Say to yourself, 'I am fuming! I feel so sad. I feel terrified…' whatever emotions are welling up, uncork them and let all of that negative energy free.

- **Echoing a response**

When someone's words are triggering you, simply repeat those words back to them. This repels the harmful words from you and gives you a chance to see them for what they are simply words. They do not define you as a person and cannot hurt you unless you let them in.

- **Family ties**

Nothing seems to trigger us more than other family members. It is as if they know exactly which buttons to press, which is why we are at our most reactive when around them. Knowing which family member triggers you the most is one way to deal with that. If you cannot avoid them, at least maintain your distance.

It is healthy to have boundaries, even with your parents, siblings, or other family members and if you feel they are crossing them, you should not allow that. Explain calmly why being with them is making you feel so bad and maintain your mental and physical space.

- **Seeking help**

When you have suffered serious trauma in the past, it can be very difficult to cope with the fallout of that all by yourself. There are many people you can turn to for help who are trained in this kind of emotional stress using different techniques, like somatic therapy and reprocessing. Do some research on the different kinds of therapy available in your area and choose one you feel will be suitable for you.

Having your finger on the trigger

We all experience both positive and negative emotions throughout our lives, which is a good thing because if we didn't what would be the point of it all? While no one wants to feel sad, angry, or upset, these kinds of negative emotions are necessary for a healthy life. Why is that?

1. Negative emotions contrast with positive emotions. How would we experience the positives and feel so good if we didn't know what feeling bad was like?
2. Negative emotions serve an evolutionary purpose. Not only are they important for our survival (fear of oncoming wild bears is a good example!) but they also help us to grow and develop as people.

When you think of negative emotions, remember that there is an upside to them.

- Anger makes us fight problems
- Fear protects us from danger
- Sadness helps us connect with those we love
- Disgust makes us reject what is unhealthy

Fear can keep us safe, disgust alerts us to things that can potentially make us ill, and sadness can lead to compassion and empathy.

As unpleasant as these negative emotions are, they do serve a purpose, and trying to suppress them all the time doesn't always do us good.

You can track your emotions using the following chart or you can make something similar on your own using emojis. You can add the list to the notes app on your smartphone, so you always have it handy. Every time you catch yourself feeling a certain way, tick it off the chart and note what you were doing/who you were with.

After you have done this a few times, you might see some patterns emerge that will help you to identify what or who is triggering you. You should also note the positives because those emotions are equally important when you experience them. If you are listening to this book on audio, simply jot down each emotion in a notebook for you to use later.

Emotion Chart

Negative

Positive

Activity/Person

Grief

Sorrow

Heartache

Sadness

Unhappiness

Depression

Hatred

Blame

Regret

Misery

Resentment

Antagonism

Anger

Fury

Hostility

Hate

Shame

Insecurity

Awkwardness

Embarrassment

Worry

Panic

Frustration

Pessimism

Cynicism

Jealousy

Pain

Anxiety

Fear

Curiosity

Inspiration

Enthusiasm

Laughter

Amusement

Empathy

Contentment

Calmness

Serenity

Peace

Trust

Bliss

Delight

Happiness

Pleasure

Joy

Ease

Satisfaction

Fulfillment

Hopeful

Confidence

Optimism

Passion

Harmony

Excitement

Gratitude

Kindness

Affection

Love

Of course, life isn't all ups and downs. Sometimes you will feel 'neutral' emotions, which are neither good nor bad. These middle-ground feelings play a large role in Buddhist thought and are known as *adukkhama-sukha*, which means something like "not painful not pleasant". That might sound very boring but these neutral feelings can be counted as positive because they are characterized by the absence of pain and suffering.

You could say that this is a state where you simply feel serene, content, and 'in the present moment'. There is a lot to be said for the benefits of mindfulness and meditation, both of which can help you to reach this kind of state.

I'll be giving you more tips about how to learn those practices in Chapter 7, which you can begin to incorporate into your everyday life.

I hope this chapter has helped you to understand more about triggers and to appreciate that you can control your responses to them when they occur.

Like anything worth doing, it takes time to identify what switches make you feel sad or angry, but once you begin to do so, it will become easier for you to process your responses.

I sincerely wish that you can begin to 'disarm' those triggers and see them for what they are – reminders of a past that have no place in your present.

Key highlights

- **The term 'trigger' refers to any situation that provokes some kind of emotional, physical, or behavioral response.**
- **Triggers usually happen before we are even aware of them, sending our bodies into survival responses of fight, flight, or freeze.**
- **The more self-awareness we have, the more difficult it is for triggers to affect our emotional well-being.**
- **Identifying what triggers you will help you to manage your responses more effectively.**
- **By monitoring what triggers you and how you feel. It is possible to learn what they are trying to tell you.**
- **Triggers can reveal underlying issues that you need to resolve.**

6
FORGIVE AND MOVE ON

"To err is human, to forgive divine." –Alexander Pope

It might seem impossible to forgive and forget, especially if you have been hurt in the past or suffered some kind of devastating experience. Even trying to get over small things can be hard: the way someone spoke to you the other day, the things they said, and how you were treated by them.

Depending on your triggers, what might seem inconsequential to someone else could make you feel terrible. Even innocent occurrences can be misinterpreted as deliberate and spiteful if they bring back bad memories.

The truth is that if we aren't able to forgive, it is very unlikely that we can forget, never mind erase everything from our memory. It is a difficult process and not one you can manage to achieve in a day. I talked about the art of forgiveness in Chapter 2, and now want to guide you through the path from forgiveness to forgetting so that you can get on with your life.

I know that you want to leave the past behind you and to do that, you need to understand what patterns you have been applying to cope with your pain. As the opening quote of this chapter says, it is a human trait to make mistakes and do wrong but takes almost superhuman strength to practice forgiveness. Only you have the power to do that though, and that is where you need to dig deep within yourself.

Reasons why you THINK you can't forgive and forget

We have all created narratives or storylines of what happened to us in the past, much like a patchwork quilt. Whatever those narratives contain, we keep adding pieces to them as we go through life, stitching together bits of this and bits of that to create a big story about what people have done to us.

It could be the parent who neglected us, the teacher who punished us, the partner who mistreated us, or the friend who betrayed us. It might have even been by someone we didn't know, such as the driver of the car who accidentally crashed into us or the pickpocket who intentionally stole our wallet.

The first thing to remember is that all of these things happened TO you and do not define you. The second thing to bear in mind is that by going over and over these events, you are reinforcing the memories.

This constant 'stitching together' impacts how you feel when you experience something negative in your current life, as you connect your present circumstances with a past one. By clinging to these stories, you could be doing yourself more harm than good.

Confusing the past with the present

Do you feel let down by a friend that you trusted? If so, is the pain really proportional to what they did or does it go back to the time when your parents forgot to pick you up from school or when you didn't get what you wanted for Christmas? Could it be that, deep inside, you find it hard to handle disappointments or that you have deeply-embedded trust issues?

Being mad at your friend for letting you down is a reasonable reaction, although that pang of pain could be linked to something entirely different that happened years ago. As we keep adding pieces to our patchwork quilt, it gets heavier and heavier, becoming so large that it literally weighs us down and we cannot move.

We tell ourselves we are angry with someone for one thing when, in reality, we are upset about something entirely different. To overcome that emotional response, it's vital that we let go of the past.

If your partner leaves you, those feelings of rejection can pile up on top of unresolved experiences of abandonment from your childhood. You will continue the narrative of being unworthy of love (because that is how you felt way back when you were younger). All that really happened was that your partner decided to leave an adult relationship that wasn't working for them anymore, for whatever reason. If you are able to forgive the parents or carers who 'abandoned' you when young, it will be much easier to cope with your partner's decision to leave.

Separating past pain from your current situation is one way to stop the repetitive patterns that determine your emotional well-being.

Confusing forgiveness with acceptance

Do you believe that forgiving someone is the same as condoning what they did? If so, it is obvious that you cannot find it in your heart to forgive them. What if I tell you that forgiveness is more about allowing yourself to heal from the pain of past actions and find peace within yourself? The thing that happened to you in the past is a fact and no one is trying to say it isn't.

You are fully entitled to criticize the bad behavior of those people who hurt you. At the same time, holding onto that hurt is like putting up a roadblock to your future. You can't drive down the freeway and get to your destination if it is full of these and will end up stuck in congestion forever. Only you can dismantle those roadblocks by accepting the past and letting go of the hurt. Do it for your own peace of mind, and not for the other person who caused you pain.

Confusing forgiveness with vulnerability

When we get angry, we turn into fighting machines as adrenaline and cortisol rage through our bodies. The brain pumps blood away from the gut and towards the muscles in preparation for physical exertion.

Our heart rate, blood pressure, and respiration increase, with the mind becoming sharpened and focused.

We go on high alert, ready to attack or be attacked. When you cannot forgive or forget, you might actually be in a constant state of anger that you are so used to by now you don't even realize it.

Anger makes us feel strong, while the thought of forgiving someone could make us look weak and vulnerable. The problem is that holding onto anger for sustained periods of time plays havoc with your physical and mental health. You just aren't built to have high levels of stress hormones running through your system all of the time and, in the end, something has to give. The irony of it is that the longer you stay angry, the more vulnerable you are becoming as that destructive emotion eats away at your health and well-being.

When bouts of anger that are linked to the past are experienced in the present, you probably feel threatened, shaky, clench your jaw, find it difficult to control your breathing, and can behave irrationally. You are putting yourself in a very vulnerable position in that present moment and all because of a past event.

If you could let go of that resentment and see it as water under the bridge, that pattern of anger response would not arise so easily. This would enable you to handle things differently, be more in control of your responses, and walk away from any event with a sense of power. Doesn't that sound much better?

Feeling sorry for yourself

Have you become used to feeling sorry for yourself because of what happened to you? This kind of victim mentality can be debilitating because it may lead you to assume that life in general is unfair. You could have gotten into the habit of seeking the attention of others to soothe your pain and this kind of external bandaid can be quite addictive.

Forgiveness means getting out of that victim mentality and realizing that the 'poor me' motto you have adopted is stopping you from moving on with your life.

How often do you tell yourself that bad things always happen to you, that life never goes your way, or that you never get what you want? The victim mentality you have fallen into will keep you feeling victimized, even if this isn't the case at all. Apart from that, obsessing over an injustice done to you or claiming the universe is against you makes it difficult for others to be compassionate, and the attention you seek will soon dry up.

Everyone suffers from bad luck, pain, heartache, and problems in life and the way to avoid those events becoming a rope around our necks is to move on from them.

You can begin to change this mindset by taking ownership of your actions in the here and now, and deciding what is really important to you. Rather than using up your energy on complaining or blaming, start taking care of your needs and forget about what others do.

When you stop pointing the finger at someone for the way you are feeling, you can begin to assume responsibility for your life and be more motivated.

No one should be allowed to steal your power from you so don't let anyone have that privilege. And most of all, change the narrative. Sure, you have had a hard time, but you will only make yourself feel worse if you keep going on and on about what happened to you, your cursed life, that everyone is out to get you, and so on.

It's like drinking poison and hoping that the other person dies, which is totally self-destructive.

Thinking that if you forgive someone, you have to face them

Forgiveness is about you, not the other person. It's not about reconciliation, appeasement, or making up with someone who has done you wrong.

You don't have to take into consideration what they feel or think. They don't even need to be privy to what you feel or think of them and there is no need to face them about it if you don't want to.

If you are waiting for someone to apologize, that can also entrap you in a kind of limbo. On the inside, you believe that if they say sorry for something they did to you, you will feel better. I can assure you that apologies, if forthcoming, do not always make you feel better. More often than not, they feed our desire to vent our bitterness at the perpetrator.

At the same time, what if you never receive that apology? Will you be doomed to feel miserable forever after because of that? Here's the thing: you cannot control what other people do but you CAN control how you live your life. Apology or not, it is possible to forgive and find your inner peace.

Being afraid of what emotions will rise if you try to forgive

If you recall from Chapter 2, forgiveness involves several stages, moving from grief to acceptance. In your attempts to go through this process, you could be worried that the emotions likely to come up will be painful and even unbearable.

That is one of the reasons why many people fail to deal with what happened to them and prefer to keep everything bottled up instead. But repressing emotions like sadness and anger is not healthy for you. The longer you avoid them, the greater the long-term effects will be so it is definitely better to let them out.

A good therapist will be able to help you do this in a safe, supportive way if you do not feel able to confront those emotions by yourself and I recommend you seek out expert help if this is the case.

Confusing forgiving with forgetting

There is no magic pill you can take to forget your past, although, as we already know, memory is a peculiar thing. It isn't always correct and is often very bad at accurately recalling information. Nevertheless, your experiences of being wronged or hurt in life can be extremely difficult to forget. That isn't necessarily a bad thing, as these experiences can teach us things about who we are and shape our values.

They may even enable personal growth and resilience, making you stronger and more able to deal with challenges in life. I wouldn't want anyone to have to go through something terrible just to learn a lesson but, as we all know, life can be hard and bad things do happen. The point is: what can we learn from these incidents?

You can work toward a stance of forgiveness without feeling that you have to forget. The memories can help you to avoid getting into a similar painful scenario and avoid people who mean you harm.

They can also make you have more empathy for others and be able to understand their problems. Forgiveness is about forgetting the pain, not the event itself.

You just aren't ready to forgive

The heart works to its own timeline and there is no rule to say you should forgive by this or that date. Maybe you will never be ready to forgive and that is fine, too. Instead of focusing on that, it will be better if you can keep looking forward and seeking ways to practice self-care.

The moment of forgiveness may just come of its own accord. When it does, you will immediately feel lighter, more serene, and happier.

You might feel like you have forgiven someone, only to be triggered months later by something you see or hear, and feel the pain again associated with your past. It is natural to experience these ups and downs so don't be too hard on yourself.

You are always evolving, changing, and learning as you go through life and there is no need to worry that you will never be able to forgive. Let time work its magic for you.

Practical steps to help you move on

Once again, I want to stress that if you suffered from a severely traumatic experience or feel unable to cope today, my first suggestion is to see a specialist who is qualified to help you with your problems. The advice contained below offers some practical tips to incorporate into your daily life to help you on your journey. They are not intended to be a cure for all emotional and physical problems associated with traumatic past experiences but can go a long way to helping you cope.

Talk through your feelings

A problem shared is a problem halved, which is why talking to someone you trust can be very helpful. In order to forgive and forget, it is important to know what feelings you are really dealing with. Putting them into words can bring a lot of clarity.

It might be uncomfortable for you to openly talk about those painful emotions but by doing so, you will be better able to identify them and disarm them.

Even if you don't want to go into all the details, a supportive ear can prove to be just what you need to process some of those feelings and eventually begin to heal.

Find the positive side

No one believes that when they go through some kind of unpleasant experience there can be anything positive about it. That is understandable, although there might be occasions where the event brings certain kinds of benefits. You might not be able to see them now but, in time, they will become more obvious.

If, for example, you discover your partner has been cheating on you, nothing can be more painful. After the initial shock and feeling of betrayal, it could be that you realize they weren't the one for you anyway and that your relationship wasn't working. Infidelity may not be the ideal way to learn this, but it can open your eyes to the reality of your situation. In that case, it could have been the best thing that ever happened to you.

Even when you can't identify a clear benefit to getting hurt by someone, you can try embracing compassion and understanding for what they did. Perhaps they had their own personal issues to work through and weren't able to act appropriately. Their behavior may have been based on some negative experiences they had in their past and even though you can't condone their actions, you could discover you are better off without them in the long run.

Begin by forgiving small things

When you can't seem to forgive something major, how about forgiving small acts instead? Let's say your friend didn't show up for your lunch appointment or a colleague forgot to remind you about an important meeting. Perhaps your friend ran into a serious problem and maybe your colleague is overworked or has too much going on in their personal life.

If you can overlook these small 'inconveniences' and see the bigger picture, the easier it will be for you to practice compassion. This approach will lead you to nurture the act of forgiving so that you are more equipped to respond with grace when wrongly done by.

Forgive yourself more often

How often in a single day do you beat yourself up for something you did or didn't do? Forgot to pay your car insurance? Didn't kiss your partner goodbye in the morning when you left home? Shouted at your kids because they seemed to be making too much noise? We all do things we shouldn't and that is part of being human.

But torturing yourself about them afterward is soul-destroying. It is much more beneficial to say, "I made a mistake. I forgive myself," and then set about rectifying the situation.

Blaming yourself for not being perfect is a fool's game that you will never win. After all, who is perfect in this life? A much kinder approach is to have some self-compassion and accept that you are human.

When you can practice self-forgiveness, it frees you from the negative mindset that makes you feel guilty and unworthy. It also allows you to forgive others more easily instead of holding grudges against them.

The act of forgiving

When you are ready to forgive someone for something they did to you, you don't need to involve them. Remember that forgiveness begins and ends with you and it is possible to forgive regardless of your relationship with the other person. Below you will find some practical yet effective ways to begin:

- **Write a letter.** Writing a letter to the person who harmed you can be very cathartic. As you address them, you can explain how you feel and tell them you have reached a point in your life where you are ready to forgive them.

It is important to remember that you do not need to send this letter to the person you are addressing. It is more like a one-sided speech you can share without being interrupted and it is your chance to have your say. It is also a wonderful way to exorcize those ghosts that have been haunting you for so long and to clear your mind of any negativity.

If you wish to physically send the letter to your wrongdoer, think very carefully about what response you would like to get back. Bear in mind that your expectations may not be met and that entering into a dialogue with this person could prolong the hurt you feel. The person involved may even have passed away or be unreachable, in which case you will never get a response. The whole point of the letter is a way to express your forgiveness, even if you know it will never be read by the person in question.

- Share your thoughts with someone. It can be a major block to healing if you aren't able to express your forgiveness, which is why you can simply share your decisions with a close friend or family member. Whoever you choose, it should be someone who understands what you have been through and can recognize the significance of your decision to forgive. Declaring your decision to move on can also commit you to the process and hearing yourself say, "I forgive…" is truly liberating.

Strategies for moving forward

Most therapeutic strategies for forgiveness are based on scientific research[1] and are usually carried out with the help of an expert because they are qualified to offer the best guidance. One method you may want to consider is REACH, which is an acronym that involves the process of:

- **R**ecalling the hurt and visualizing the experience
- **E**mpathizing with the wrongdoer without minimizing their actions
- **A**ltruism, or looking at forgiveness as a gift you would like to give
- **C**ommitting to forgiveness by writing or telling about your decision
- **H**olding onto forgiveness by making a written note that you did forgive and referring to it when needed.

You can learn to REACH forgiveness by working with the hurt that you might have suffered. I have provided some prompts for you below to respond to in your own time that focus on your feelings and motivations about anything you are dealing with.

It is a good idea to begin with a minor event, rather than something far too traumatic to face yet. For example, think about the last time someone was rude to you or let you down, or the occasion when you felt hurt by someone's behavior and still find it difficult to forgive them.

1. Can you describe the event?

2. Make a brief note of how you felt and reacted to the event after that.

3. Describe anything that has happened relating to the event since then that has affected your current feelings and motivations.

4. Imagine that someone you know stole from you. What would your current thoughts and feelings be about that person? Use the scale 1 2 3 4 5 (strongly disagree, mildly disagree, agree, and mildly agree or strongly agree):

1. I'll make them pay.

2. I hope something bad happens to them.

3. I want them to get what they deserve.

4. I'm going to get even.

5. I want to see them hurt and miserable.

6. I'm going to keep as much distance as possible from them.

7. I'll live as if they don't exist.

8. I won't trust anyone again.

9. I would find it hard to be nice to them in the future.

10. I'd rather avoid them.

11. I'd cut off the relationship with them.

12. I would withdraw from them.

13. I would look for the reason behind their actions.

14. I would take steps toward reconciliation by writing, calling, texting, or expressing my concern to them.

15. I would make an effort to be nicer and more concerned about them.

16. I would do my best to put aside the mistrust.

17. I would try to make amends.

18. I would be willing to forget the past and concentrate on the present.

19. Even though their actions hurt me, I would still have goodwill for them.

20. I would put the event behind me and move forward with our relationship.

21. Despite what they did, I would want us to continue our relationship.

22. I would let go of my hurt and resentment.

23. Although they hurt me, I would put the hurt aside.

24. I would forgive them for what they did to me.

25. I would have to let go of my anger so I could work on restoring our relationship.

It is a difficult transition to go from being bitter and angry to reaching total forgiveness. You might only be able to reach the stage of granting forgiveness, even though you no longer want to continue a relationship with that person.

That is different from emotional forgiveness, where you truly let go of the negative emotions toward the person who harmed you and even feel more positive about them. Only you can make that transitional journey and you have to do it at your own pace. With each step you make, you will begin to feel better about yourself and that is the important thing.

Find your own example of forgiveness.

Can you think of a classic example where the victim chooses to forgive the transgressor? It may be a story from a children's book, a movie plot, or a religious parable. Why did the offender commit the act and why did the victim choose to forgive them? In which way did the act of forgiveness bring closure to the story?

If you can't think of a story, real life is full of them. After a quick search on the internet, I found many inspiring stories about ordinary people who underwent something dreadful that were able to forgive those responsible.

There's the woman out shopping for Halloween candy at her local mall to give to underprivileged children. She was hit by a shopping cart pushed from the second-story by two young boys[2].

After suffering a serious brain injury, losing the sight in her left eye, being in a temporary coma, and undergoing weeks of physical therapy, she later stated that she held no ill-will against the boys and wished them well.

Another true event was the inspiration for a movie called, 'Just Let Go'.[3] A man and his family were hit by a 17-year-old drunk driver while in their car. Unfortunately, both his 11-year-old son and 9-year-old daughter were killed outright, as well as his pregnant wife.

He went on to publicly forgive his family's killer and today is a motivational speaker, sharing his story of healing and forgiveness with others.

The above incidents are prime examples of how we can reach a place of forgiveness, even when suffering terrible loss and grief. It takes a big heart to accomplish that but, more significantly, the victims forgave the people who caused them harm so they could find peace within themselves.

Practice releasing the burden of unforgiveness.

Here is a simple exercise you can do to release yourself from the burden of being unable to forgive.

- Clasp your hands and extend your arms out as far as you can.
- Imagine that you hold in your hands all the weight of unforgiveness.
- Hold your clenched hands outstretched for thirty seconds.
- As your arms begin to grow tired, think of everything else you could be doing with your hands (and with your life) if you were able to let go and move on.
- Remember that it is hurting you, not your offender, to hold on to this burden.
- Even if you are not ready to 'let go', open your hands and let your arms drop to your sides.
- Notice the relief you experience and imagine the same feeling you will have when you are ready to forgive.

Wash your hands of the past

This is another simple exercise you can do on your path to releasing yourself from the pain of past experiences.

- Take a pen and write on the palm of your hand a very brief description of what happened to you. You can even just write the words 'hurt' or 'pain' if you like.
- Now, go to the bathroom and begin to wash the word(s) off your hand.
- You may not be able to get the ink off at first but keep trying.
- The more often you wash your hands, the sooner the ink will eventually be erased.

- You will eventually become free of those negative, unforgiving feelings.

Choose your emotions

Find a photo or picture that always makes you smile and place it somewhere you will see it often. It might be of your friends, family, or an image you found on the internet. The point of this exercise is to show you that you do have a choice about how you feel.

When you look at the picture, you want to smile and you don't want to feel down at that moment. In the same way, you can choose to hold onto painful memories and emotions or replace them with love and compassion.

Another simple exercise is to draw a picture showing a before and after representation of how you feel once you have let go of the past. What do your before and after pictures look like and what are the differences between the two? What has changed in the way you feel now that you can see what letting go can bring you?

Who are your heroes?

Think back over your life and identify those people who you knew personally or have heard of who are your forgiveness heroes. Pick out one person who you consider to be very forgiving and explain why. It may be a historical figure such as Jesus, Gandhi, or Martin Luther King, Jr., or a group of people like victims of war crimes. What qualities do you think make them a good example for all of us? Usually, we admire those who were able to forgive because we know it is such a difficult thing to do. That makes it all the more worthwhile.

Deciding to try to forgive

Can you bring to mind an event that really hurt you and make a decision right now to try to forgive?

Can you commit to trying to experience the freedom of emotionally forgiving?

Do you want to try to forgive and stick by your decision?

Do you want to try to experience feeling better after forgiveness?

If so, you can fill out this Forgiveness Contract. If you are listening to this book on audio, simply copy it onto a piece of paper and fill in the blanks.

Forgiveness Contract

I declare to myself that I intend to try to forgive (insert name of person who caused you harm)_____ and I also want to become a more forgiving person.

_____ Name (Signature)

_____ Witness (Signature - Optional)

Moving on

You may be able to forgive but can't forget, and that's OK. Even when your memories linger, forgiveness will eventually allow you to move forward. In the meantime, try to focus on the good things in your life and express gratitude for them every day. Pay more attention to the wonderful things happening around you and simply enjoy the gift of living on this beautiful planet.

Stop thinking that everything that happens has some deeper meaning or is because of fate. It is up to you to give meaning to your life, no matter what challenges you face along the way. Allow yourself to break free of the bonds that stunt your emotional growth and practice self-care as often as possible so you can mature, flourish, and move on.

The past is but a memory. Store it deep in the archive if you can't delete it entirely. Then, just forget about it as you work toward your own happiness.

Key highlights

- **Believing you cannot forgive is at the heart of your inability to do so.**
- **Confusing the past with the present keeps you stuck there.**

- **Forgiving someone is not the same as forgetting what they did to you.**
- **It isn't a weakness to accept your past and it doesn't make you vulnerable.**
- **Forgiveness is about finding your inner peace and has nothing to do with the person who wronged you.**
- **The act of forgiveness begins once you commit to moving on.**
- **Declaring to forgive will lead you to a brighter future.**

7
MOVING INTO THE LIGHT

"*The power for creating a better future is contained in the present moment: You create a good future by creating a good present.*"
–Eckhart Tolle

Life is like a river, always changing and moving forward. When you refuse to move on or seem unable to, you can get stuck in a deep, dark, stagnant pool of damaging emotions. I know that isn't the place you want to be and that you would love to come up for air, breathe, and float effortlessly toward the light.

To do that, you have to make a decision now. The place you find yourself in at this moment may not be serving you anymore. It might feel heavy, painful, and lonely. The future is full of brightness and new experiences, just there for the taking. After all, life is about living, not standing still, so how can you begin that transition and hope for better days ahead?

I won't lie to you. Sometimes we have to go through difficult and often painful events to truly appreciate what we have. It can take a long time for each one of us to pull ourselves out of a dark period and often we just have to go through it so we can work out what the lesson was.

I remember struggling to deal with a relationship that ended in heartache in the past. I was very young and thought I had found my 'one true love'. Of course, it didn't last, and it took me a good two years to get over it. Being a heartbroken teenager, I thought I would never feel good enough about myself again or be able to move on.

This kind of thing must happen to millions of people all over the globe but at the time, I felt as if this was only happening to me.

When it comes to romantic relationships, we tend to plan our whole lives around that person and when they let us down, it can feel like the end of the world. Apart from the agony of pain and rejection, we start believing we aren't good enough, or that we did something wrong. Disappointment and despair are difficult emotions to get over, especially when everything around you is a painful reminder of that person.

It is normal to grieve for any loss, be that romantic or otherwise, especially if you are a highly sensitive person.

But you need to go on because living in limbo is unhealthy and takes a big chunk out of your life. How long do you think it is permissible to feel miserable? Six months, a year, two, a lifetime? Isn't that such a waste?

If you can relate to this, you need to see what your current state is costing you and make the decision to transition to something better. Rather than sitting in the darkness, seek out the light at the end of the tunnel and leave the past behind you.

Welcome to positivity

Instead of dwelling on the negatives, focusing on the positives is much better for you. Sometimes we have to get up and search for positivity though, as it isn't always forthcoming, especially if we have been feeling down for a long time.

Positivity is more than just feeling happy: it is a way of interpreting our lives and everything we experience – even the bad things. To cultivate positivity, we must constantly pay attention to our emotions and thoughts, and be prepared to tweak them as we go.

In doing so, we can learn to grow a positive mindset that is useful when anything happens in our interactions with others, and when we are alone. We can make the decision to act with positivity and get used to responding to any situation that crops up with the same optimism.

Being negative can be a useful emotion sometimes as it helps you to understand what has gone wrong and what lessons can be learned.

On the other hand, holding on to it once it has served its purpose can seriously affect your well-being and physical health. It also becomes a burden that you carry around with you, thinking you need it like some kind of shell to crawl into when you want to protect yourself. In reality, carrying negativity breeds unhappiness and dissatisfaction, preventing you from being able to enjoy life to the full.

You can make a decision right now to be more positive, even if you aren't 100% ready to take it on board fully. Choose from one of the following statements below to begin with that best describes how you feel in this present moment:

- Yes, I have taken the decision to be more positive.
- Although I have decided to be more positive, I'm not sure if I'll be able to manage it in the future.
- No, I haven't decided to be positive just yet.
- At the moment, I can't see how positivity is going to help me.

If this decision seems hard for you to make now, do you have any idea why that is? What comes into your mind when you read about being positive in the future? What doubts and fears are holding you back in a negative mindset? What needs to change for you to begin to see things more positively?

Making a decision to welcome positivity into your life doesn't mean that you will automatically feel any different. It's one thing to set your mind on it and quite another to suddenly wake up feeling full of the joys of spring. These positive emotions will come gradually because they will be reinforced by your actions and what perspectives you take in the future.

You may often see inspirational quotes on social media telling you to, 'Be positive!' but it really isn't that simple. You need to slowly transition from the negative darkness of the past to the positive brightness of the future and it can't happen overnight. For that reason, be patient with yourself and put your trust in the process.

Five steps for a positive future

Adopt a meaningful outlook

If you truly wish to stop worrying and having negative thoughts, you have to break the cycle. To do this:

- Think of one meaningful thing that came out of a bad situation you experienced. Perhaps you learned a valuable lesson or realized the importance of something.
- Write down one positive event in your life and read it over several times. Whenever negative thoughts creep in, recall this positive event and keep it at the forefront of your mind.
- Embrace the endless possibilities of life that lie ahead of you. Who knows what could happen in the future: a new job, a new partner, a cure for an illness that is affecting you, a chance to acquire something precious… The list is endless, and these are all things you might not expect or even think are possible now. In reality, you never know what the future will bring and that is an exciting thought!
- Acknowledge that you have been through hard times but now you have to move beyond them. Every morning when you wake up, you can say to yourself, *"Yesterday is my past and today is my future."*

Recognize your strengths

Everyone has strengths but it is easy to forget about them when you have been a victim or suffered a bad trauma. When you are at your lowest, you won't feel particularly brave or strong. That's why it is a good idea to remind yourself of the qualities you possess and acknowledge how important they are.

Martin Seligman[1], Ph.D., and Neal Mayerson, Ph.D., were the first to define the positive character strengths that all people have to varying degrees and you will find them listed below. They are divided into six classes of virtues: wisdom, courage, humanity, justice, temperance, and transcendence. Take a look and think about how many of them you believe you possess in each category:

Wisdom:

- Creativity
- Curiosity
- Open-mindedness
- Love of learning
- Perspective

Courage:

- Honesty
- Bravery
- Persistence
- Zest

Humanity

- Kindness
- Love
- Social intelligence

Justice

- Fairness
- Leadership
- Teamwork

Temperance

- Forgiveness

- Modesty
- Prudence
- Self-regulation

Transcendence

- Appreciation of beauty
- Gratitude
- Hope
- Humor
- Religiousness/spirituality

If you had to choose only five of the strengths above that define your character, which ones would they be? Each and every one of us has strengths but we don't always recognize them.

This failure to use what we have often means we also fail to act with positivity because the negative beliefs we have about ourselves are so entrenched within our mindsets.

Identifying your strengths can be very liberating as it means you aren't held back by fear of not achieving your goals. When you deal with hurdles or challenges in life, knowing and believing that you can overcome them will open up a world of possibilities.

Some strengths are particularly empowering when it comes to being positive about the future and it will be helpful if you can nurture them more. I want you to think about the last time you did something that reflected the following strengths. Make a note of which ones you recall and remind yourself of what happened in each particular situation:

1. You acted with compassion – you sympathized with others going through a tough situation
2. You practiced forgiveness – you were able to replace negative feelings like revenge and grudge-bearing with positive feelings of understanding
3. You acted with altruism – you did something good for others, even if there was no direct benefit to yourself

4. You practiced patience – you were able to wait and delay gratification without getting frustrated
5. You were humble – you were able to see yourself realistically in the bigger picture and value all people and situations
6. You acted with courage – you went through a scary situation because you knew it was for the greater good
7. You expressed love – you held someone in positive regard unconditionally, without putting limits on your relationship with them
8. You practiced fairness – you did something right or just
9. You practiced abstinence – you kept yourself from doing something negative or that would have negative consequences
10. You were open-minded – you could see the good in situations that you would normally frown upon or criticize
11. You practiced perseverance – you didn't give up and persisted until you achieved your goal
12. You were level headed – you kept your emotions in check when making an important decision or when dealing with a difficult situation
13. You practiced cooperation – you were able to peacefully work or collaborate with others

How many of the above did you note down? Even one is fantastic because now you know that you can exercise that strength. I am sure you have many more so keep referring to this checklist and tick off any new strengths you become aware of when the situation arises.

Put things into perspective

We often distance ourselves from others when we are feeling negative about life, and this can eventually make us feel worse about ourselves. If you are in that mindset, you might find it difficult to have a realistic perspective on things and probably always imagine the 'worst-case scenario'.

This is when you are unable to envisage a positive outcome and tend to 'catastrophize any situation.

I have a friend who is exactly like this, imagining the worst-case scenario even when there is no logical reason to assume that things will go wrong. Her perspective is completely clouded by the feelings of negativity she has about herself and life in general. Sadly, she lost her father in a tragic air crash when she was around 8 years old and this has definitely colored her view on life. As a consequence, she will never take any risks, step out of her comfort zone, or even do simple things like travel or try out a new restaurant. In her eyes, everything will turn out to be a disaster.

She also finds it difficult to set goals or make future plans, fearing that they will never come to fruition.

That's a very sad way to live and I feel for her. In her eyes, the present and future are still being shaped by a terrible accident that happened over forty years ago and, until she can work through it, she will continue to think this way.

Hopefully, she will one day be able to reach a place of acceptance and change her perceptions of life so she can begin to live it to the fullest.

When you find yourself saying things like: "It's never going to work, He's not going to make it, I will probably fail,", consider where those negative perspectives are coming from. Are they realistic, probable, or even rational? Very often, they are manifestations of our negative thought patterns we take for granted and have nothing to do with the reality of the situation.

One of the major aspects of positivity is realizing just how good it is for you. An easy way to achieve that is by counting your blessings and giving gratitude. These are such simple things to do but so effective because they help you to gain a better perspective on life.

Good things happen as well as bad, and when you remind yourself of that every day, it is easier to gradually shift from a negative mindset to one of positivity and hope.

Can you list ten things you are grateful for in your life? You could, for example, be grateful for your good health, for having a roof over your head, or for a well-paid job. You will be surprised at how many things you have to be grateful for when you really think about it. Have a go, and write down anything that comes to mind, no matter how small:

I am grateful for:

1

2

3

4

5

6

7

8

9

10

Now that you have thought about everything you are grateful for in life, can you think of five more things you would like to savor in the future?

Savoring is when you slow down to really appreciate something and take in all of the pleasure it brings you. Imagine trying out a new kind of cuisine, visiting an exotic destination, climbing a high mountain, buying your first home, or anything else you would like to do.

There is a reason why people say, 'Savor the moment,' and it has to do with creating a positive experience that you will recall well into the future.

Gratitude and savoring are essential if you want to move on and enjoy your life because they fill you with enjoyment, enthusiasm, and hope. They also help you to find emotional balance and well-being, despite what has gone on in your past. They offer a future full of brightness, positivity, and fulfillment.

Follow your passions

Now that I have reminded you of all the wonderful things in your life, how about considering what you want? What dreams and goals do you have? What fills you with excitement and enthusiasm when you think about it? What can you look forward to that will bring you satisfaction? Can you think of three things?

Whatever it is that fires you up with enthusiasm, write it down and set yourself the task of doing it more often. If your passion is sport, for example, make a plan to play more, join a team, become better at it, and invite your friends to come along with you. If you love music, learn to play an instrument, make your own playlist, and listen to music wherever you go. As you begin to do the things you love more often, you will be more engaged in your present and have greater optimism about your future.

There is nothing keeping you from looking forward apart from your mindset. You do have a choice about how you see yourself in one, five, or ten years time and you can even control what tomorrow will bring. You can either hold onto your negative thoughts or replace them with positive ones by recognizing your strengths and being grateful for what you have.

Dedicate yourself to being a more positive person

Make the decision to be positive. Why not decide today to be more positive about your future? To do this, you can begin by answering some simple questions:

1. Why do you want to be a more positive person? Think of as many reasons as you can.
2. Who are your positivity heroes?
3. What makes them so positive?
4. What are the 3 most positive experiences you have had in your life?
5. What 3 things are you hopeful about in your future?
6. If you write a letter of positivity to your future self, what would you like to tell them?

Stop grieving. It is OK to feel aggrieved about whatever has happened to you and you are entitled to go through emotions of bitterness or pain.

At some point though, you have to say, 'Enough is enough,' and let the hurt go. Getting things out of your system can be extremely helpful and you can do this through journaling or by talking to a friend. Both of these can help you to find perspective and adopt a different viewpoint.

Forgive yourself for any mistakes you believe you have made and, if it is appropriate, try to make amends with others if you want to find inner peace.

Set new goals that are realistic and achievable. This will help you to concentrate on what is ahead and be more animated about the possibilities. Write your goals down and think about how each one can be achieved. What can you do today to begin realizing them? Make sure they are achievable and realistic, and set yourself a deadline by which you want to have reached them.

Think about what your priorities are. Is family important to you, your career, or perhaps your physical health? Knowing what means the most to you can steer you toward new activities or actions that help you realize your future plans. If you desire to spend more time with your family, what do you need to change in your daily life?

If you want to advance your career, what new skills should you make the effort to learn? Your priorities may shift over time as your circumstances change and that is fine. As long as you keep your priorities at the forefront of your actions and stay true to yourself, you can't go wrong.

Think about your legacy. Far from being a morbid idea, thinking about what you wish to leave behind can be a great motivator to spur you into action. A legacy can be anything, from your reputation to acts of kindness and it is how you would like to be remembered by others. Everything you do from now on can contribute to building your legacy and it is a good idea to begin by writing down what you would like that to be.

Once you have done that, think of ways that will enable you to live in alignment with your wishes.

Your legacy may be that you want to be remembered as a good person, for example. If so, find avenues that allow you to practice this such as through voluntary work. Remember that creating a legacy is about more than just doing good so you can receive praise or admiration.

It is about living in alignment with your values and finding real fulfillment.

Take time out. You need to spend some time relaxing, especially when you live in a culture that tells you to keep busy. Work hard but play hard too, as this will help you to maintain that all-important work/life balance.

Relaxation is just as important as being productive for your mental, physical, and emotional health and you don't have to feel guilty about it.

Make a point of allocating time each day to unwind and do something relaxing, whether that is reading, walking, meditating, or simply sitting quietly. Allow yourself to switch off from the outside world for a while, close the notifications on your phone, and take a break from the hustle and bustle.

Go for a weekend away or just a day at the beach and reconnect with nature, which can be wonderful therapy for the soul.

Practice mindfulness. Mindfulness is the basic human ability to be fully present, aware of where you are and what you are doing, without overreacting or being overwhelmed by what's going on around us.

Being fully present in the moment has been proven to help nurture self-realization and emotional control. Anyone can learn how to access mindfulness and you don't need to have any special training or be of a particular religious persuasion.

The reason mindfulness is so empowering is that it can help you to stay grounded and emotionally balanced by disarming an over-active mind that can often cause confusion and pain.

You can practice mindfulness anywhere, any time, and don't need any special equipment. It involves stopping what you are doing, closing your eyes, and allowing yourself to experience the present moment.

It may take some getting used to if you are always over-thinking and fixating on certain aspects of your life but after trying it a few times, you will soon see how beneficial it can be in 'quieting the mind'.

Follow these easy instructions when you try to practice mindfulness for the first time:

- Sit very still and close your eyes.
- As thoughts enter your mind (which they inevitably will) simply allow them to be there without trying to negate them.
- As you observe these thoughts, be an impartial witness to them without feeling the need to judge.
- Be aware of your tendency to want to judge them or react to them.
- Accept that your thoughts are unfolding and be patient until they pass by.
- Remain open and curious about any emotions you feel at this time without the need for self-criticism.
- Know that it is OK for these emotions to arise and simply allow them to subside.
- You only have to be yourself in this present moment and there is no need to change anything.
- As you become more aware of your inner experience, you may also notice certain thoughts and feelings that you are trying to hold onto.
- Allow them to be released without any force or pressure.
- Open your eyes. You will feel calmer and more relaxed.

The act of mindfulness may seem difficult at first, but the more often you do it, the easier it becomes. It is like watching clouds pass by in the sky that you have no control over. They appear, then float away, leaving a clarity that you will find useful when life brings you challenges in the future.

A few minutes of mindfulness every day can really keep the painful past away and offer you a future of inner peace and calm.

Add meaning to your life

A life without meaning is a life wasted and I believe that we are all here to contribute something unique. Finding meaning in your life can help you to move forward, fueled by a greater sense of drive and determination. When you feel lost and despondent, bringing meaning into your life will give you direction and a sense of purpose, which is very important to your overall well-being.

When you discover your purpose, you will be compelled to make the most of your abilities and even make an impact on someone else's life. You might need to try out different things before you discover what it is that fulfills you.

You could find that satisfaction in your job, especially if it is also a vocation, such as being a teacher or doctor. Maybe you want to help others and contribute your time to a local charity or a greater cause. Perhaps life has more meaning for you when you express your creative side and draw, write, or build things with your hands. Life can be so much more satisfying when you live with purpose and meaning so think about what you would like to pursue so you can achieve that goal. Here are some pointers to guide you:

What are your strengths and talents?

How could you use these to help others?

What activities fill you with a sense of joy, pleasure, and purpose?

What activities motivate you and fill you with positive energy?

What would make you happy?

What does purposeful living mean to you?

What could bring more quality to your life?

Each question is food for thought and there are no right or wrong answers. You can choose anything that is aligned with your needs, desires, and values. When you have a reason to get up in the morning, all of your mental and emotional energy is channeled toward that, leaving you little time to focus on the past. You become fully engaged in achieving something meaningful and this is a healthy way to build a more rewarding future.

I hope you already feel pumped and ready for action!

Erasing the past

It might not be possible to completely wipe out painful memories, but you can spend less time focusing on them. Remember that what you do now in the present can define your future but carrying the burden of the past around with you won't get you very far.

It is a lot healthier to dream about the future than it is to dwell on the past and you can do that by making some simple adjustments to your thinking.

Make new memories

Painful memories are hard to delete but when you begin making new, happier memories, your brain's storage system will archive anything that you do not need. Making new memories isn't just about having pleasant experiences and hoping they will stick, so we need to do some work to make sure they become embedded well enough in the place of old ones.

1. Pay attention

The easiest way to store new memories is to be mindful when you are feeling happy. This involves savoring the moment and paying attention to what you are experiencing at that time. It is through attention that our memories are made. If you don't notice something, you aren't likely to remember it.

But if you focus on a specific thing, you are more likely to hold onto it. Being in a heightened state of awareness occurs when we are in a state of fear, which is why bad experiences can last in our memory bank for so long.

If we apply that awareness to a positive event, that too will find its place in our memory store. It's like taking a mental snapshot of what is happening to you so you can carry it around with you and look at it when you want to.

2. Build 'episodic' memories using all of your senses

When you take that mental snapshot of a happy moment, absorb the experience with all of your senses. Pay attention to the sounds and aromas that make up the scene, as well as what you see. This helps you to build up what is known as 'episodic memories' that you can later recall.

You might, for example, remember the smell of the turkey on Thanksgiving, the sound of laughter, or a certain piece of music. The memory is wrapped up in a feeling that helps to create warmer, more vivid recollections of the experience that you can revisit and relive.

3. Try something new

Everyone remembers their first kiss, but few will recall the countless kisses after that. This is because we tend to remember our first-time experiences much better than things we do over and over again. Imagine, for example, commuting on the same route to work every day. After a while, you may not even remember how you got there at all because it doesn't leave any impression on your brain anymore.

That is why seeking out new, novel experiences is a great way to create new memories. Do something new, try your hand at anything you haven't done before, visit somewhere different, or a new sport a go. You can create brand new memories that will stick in your mind and oust the old ones you do not need anymore.

4. Build memory triggers into your day

Memory works by association and when you smell roast beef, it may remind you of a particular time and place when roast beef was part of the scenario. The way to use this ability to your advantage is by turning everyday objects into mementos. Let's say you wear the same shoes when taking your dog for a walk in the park.

Every time you see the shoes, they will remind you of your adorable companion and give you a warm feeling inside. By associating specific objects or even places with times happily spent, you can help to blend those memories into the story of your life.

Equally, get rid of objects that trigger painful memories and withdraw from relationships that remind you of bad experiences. Create space for new memories to emerge that you will be able to reminisce on in the future.

5. Reminisce on good times

Once you have stored those happy memories, keep recalling them to stop them from fading. Like the muscles in your body that become stronger the more you use them, memories can be reinforced when you call them to mind frequently.

Create a store cupboard of happy memories that you can always open and find exactly what you are looking for. Whenever you feel overwhelmed by bad memories, open the store of good memories and select the one you need to feel better at that moment.

You may be going through a difficult time now and miss companionship, your family, or other comforts. By accessing your good memories, you can actually feel better in the present, regardless of your situation.

Closure

Closure is the process of coming to terms with something and bringing it to an end in your mind. This means that you are finally able to tie up the loose ends and move on. Closure implies acceptance of what happened and honoring the transition away from what has finished toward something new. It is about going beyond the limitations you have been putting on yourself and discovering different possibilities. To reach closure:

- You need to take full responsibility for your actions and be ready to move on.
- You need to stop holding on to anything that makes you unhappy.
- You must face up to any loss and void it may create.

When you can be honest with yourself about the reasons you have not been able to let go until now, you will clear the way for a more realistic understanding of the situation. You could go through a kind of grieving process and that is normal because you have been living a life heavily invested in the past. Change will come in good time so be patient with yourself.

Finding closure allows you to move on and be optimistic about your future. Hopefully, you will have also learned something valuable from everything you went through and come out of it stronger than ever before.

It took me many years to find closure after my father died. I was angry that he never apologized for being such a bad parent while we were growing up. I wanted him to say he was sorry or explain his actions and I felt cheated out of that opportunity when he passed away.

After several years of soul-searching and looking at the events from a place of greater compassion and self-awareness. I did find the closure I needed. It became apparent to me that he must have been a very unhappy man to have to drink so much.

Maybe the pressure or expectations put on him by life were simply too much for him to handle, and his behavior was a vent for his frustration. For whatever reason, he was unable to be a good role model and I had to accept that.

Once I accepted that, I didn't need him to apologize to me anymore. I could close that chapter of my life and move on. I also believe that I learned a lot from those childhood experiences and they helped to make me the person I am today.

I have stopped wishing that things could have been different because they can't, and nothing can change that. I don't feel any bitterness now toward my father and can say with all my heart, 'I forgive you.'

My life has since moved on and I feel happy, content, and grateful for everything I have. This is my personal journey and I hope that you can also reach inner peace after all you have suffered in the past and find closure. It is so liberating, trust me.

When you live with purpose, are mindful of your present, and store happy memories, life takes on a whole new meaning. Having closure allows a future that shines more brightly than ever before!

Key highlights

- Positivity is a powerful tool that you can benefit from once you change your mindset.
- By following the 5 steps for positivity, the present becomes more satisfying and the future seems brighter.
- Identifying your strengths stops you from being held back and helps you to achieve your goals.
- Having a positive outlook changes your perspective on your experiences.
- Working toward creating your future legacy begins today.
- Practicing mindfulness can bring greater self-awareness and an appreciation of the present moment.
- Finding meaning in your life will propel you to move forward with greater drive and determination.
- Making happy new memories will replace old negative ones.

8
LOVE YOURSELF DEEPLY

"*How you love yourself is how you teach others to love you.*"
–Rupi Kaur

If you have read my book **Love Yourself Deeply**, you will know that self-love is the most important gift you can give yourself. No matter what painful experiences you have had in the past or how difficult your present is, self-love is the one thing that can heal, protect, and fortify you. It really is a superpower and everyone has the capacity to experience it.

As an act of self-preservation, I strongly recommend that you focus on your inner needs and take the time to nurture more love for the wonderful person you are. No one else has the right to define you, make you miserable, or destroy your well-being so do not let them.

The past has past and the present moment is all you have. If you can take back control of your life, it is possible to start envisioning an optimistic future and the road to that destination begins with self-love.

Recognize your inner worth and value

Certain events in your life may have led you to feel unworthy or unlovable and you could still be carrying these misconceptions of yourself around with you.

Thinking you aren't good enough, intelligent enough, or attractive enough, are all remnants of something that someone once told you or made you feel. They aren't true, but you believe them because you have lost faith in your own sense of self.

Memories can become so ingrained in your view of yourself that, somewhere along the way, you forget who you really are. Living under the illusion that you are a certain way rather than being your true self can keep you trapped in a cage that you have flown into of your own free will. You will think and behave according to someone else's definition of who you are, instead of having an awareness of your authentic, true self.

Only you hold the key to unlocking this cage and finding true freedom and that key is self-love. If you have never thought about self-love before or assumed it to be some wishy-washy, girly idea, then think again.

It is the most empowering idea you will ever hear and, without it, you will continue to be trapped in a cycle of negativity

If you recall from the previous chapter, I asked you to pinpoint your strengths. Perhaps you could only identify one or two, which is fine. Sometimes, we are so used to identifying ourselves in one way or another that we forget what our inner qualities are.

This could be due to a lack of self-esteem, which is a classic symptom of someone who has forgotten how to love themselves.

Why self-esteem matters

When I talk about self-esteem, I am referring to the way you see yourself and includes a whole range of self-defining traits, such as:

- Self-acceptance: The ability to accept yourself as you are
- Self-compassion: The ability to treat yourself kindly and forgive yourself

- Self-respect: The belief that you deserve respect
- Self-worth: How much you value yourself
- Self-image: The perception you have of your body and yourself as a whole
- Self-confidence: The ability to behave in line with your sense of self

If these perceptions of yourself are controlled by something from your past, they will not be true representations of who you are today and need to change.

There are different levels of self-esteem: low, healthy, and excessive. We might all go through periods in our lives when we don't feel particularly confident or worthy, although that doesn't necessarily mean we are lacking in self-esteem.

Low self-esteem is usually a chronic inability to see yourself as having any value and can be affected by many factors. The way you were raised and your personality traits may come into play, as well as all the experiences that have gone into shaping your identity.

If you have suffered trauma or a long-standing painful past, it is understandable that you might struggle with refinding your authentic self. Depending on how deep the wounds go, it can take a long time for them to heal and it is important to go at your own pace.

Low self-esteem manifests itself as feelings of inadequacy, not being 'good enough', and worthlessness. If this is you, you might not like attention, want to take up as little space as possible, and have difficulty accepting compliments.

You are probably also unable to prioritize your own needs and prefer to appease the people around you. You are likely to be over-critical about yourself and very judgmental, doubt your abilities, and will avoid anything that could result in failure. Does this sound like you? If so,

- Can you pinpoint a time when you remember being treated badly, or told you were not worthy?

- Did your parents let you down on that score, or was it someone in authority, such as a teacher?
- Were you discriminated against at some point in the past because of your race, class, or economic status, or were you bullied by your schoolmates?
- Did you suffer a traumatic experience, be that of a physical, mental, or emotional nature, that had a massive impact on your feelings of self-worth?
- Have you undergone a stressful situation, such as a financial, relational, or health issue, that has slowly eroded your self-esteem?

When your self-esteem is at an all-time low, self-care is usually the last thing on your mind and it's very easy to neglect your emotional, physical, and psychological health completely. It can lead to feelings of helplessness and reluctance to change because you believe that to be impossible.

On the other hand, healthy self-esteem looks very different.

- You will celebrate who you are and can be yourself, regardless of what others may think.
- You will find it OK to be vulnerable with those you love.
- You will be assertive and able to set healthy boundaries.
- You will look for feedback from people you trust and accept failure as part of normal life.
- You will have a sound belief in your worth and are not afraid to speak up for yourself or stand up for others.

Excessive self-esteem is when you overestimate your skills, abilities, and importance, and, just like low self-esteem, can be caused by a lack of confidence or a feeling of worthlessness. Rather than these negative beliefs making you feel small, you will try to compensate for them through the way you act and what you say. You could come across to others as arrogant, impulsive, reckless, manipulative, and unable to take criticism. This is not what you should be aiming for.

To build your self-esteem so that it reaches a healthy level, there are a couple of things that will help:

Prioritize self-care. This means looking after yourself and honoring your inherent worthiness. There are plenty of things you can do to promote self-care such as getting enough sleep, eating healthily, having regular health check-ups, and avoiding harmful substances like drugs or alcohol. Self-care also includes seeing to your emotional needs, such as experiencing pleasure, companionship, and love.

Practice self-compassion. It is normal to make mistakes but forgiving yourself is a constructive act that will leave your self-esteem intact. When you can admit to a mistake and accept failure, you are exercising self-compassion and this allows you to love yourself despite falling short of your expectations or goals. Being kind to yourself is an act of true self-love.

Reject perfectionism. No one is perfect and life isn't meant to be, which is why it is better for you to set realistic goals and expectations. This way, you avoid disappointment and won't feel bad when things don't go your way. Having high expectations of yourself can lead to disappointment so approach life with more temperance and less pressure to achieve and you will manage failure much better.

Resist comparisons. I know this is difficult in the times we live in, with so many people trying to portray the ideal body, face, or lifestyle on social media. In reality, you are a unique individual with a life of your own to lead, and comparing yourself to others is counterproductive if you have low self-esteem. It is best to stay away from social media if you find it all too overwhelming and cannot help but compare yourself to others.

The benefits of positive psychology

I'm a great believer in helping ourselves to live a happier, more meaningful life, and know that Positive Psychology can be very beneficial. This particular strand of self-help was founded around the 1990s by Dr. Martin Seligman, President of the American Psychological Association, and it focuses on mental wellness as a path to living a more fulfilling life.

When talking about self-love, there are many benefits to using some of the ideas found in Positive Psychology, which is based on four basic tenets:

1. Eudaimonia (The Good Life)

This is an idea going back to ancient Greece which correlates with a profound form of wellness, contentment, joy, and satisfaction. We all want to experience those feelings, right? When you nurture self-love, that becomes possible whereas, when you ignore your needs, it is extremely hard to access these positive feelings and experiences.

2. Surviving vs. Flourishing

If your psychological well-being is seen as a spectrum, *surviving* is lacking in color because it involves illness, disorders, and trauma. On the other hand, *flourishing* is a vibrant color that portrays not only the ability to survive but to thrive and grow as well. You can overcome the challenges you face in life when you feel strong, sure of yourself, and believe in your potential, all of which come from self-love. Becoming a person who is living their best life is possible if you can make that transition from merely surviving to truly flourish.

3. Flow

In Positive Psychology, flow is that state of immersive activity when you are fully engaged in something you love doing. It's like being 'in the zone' and not getting distracted by any negative thoughts. When you experience flow, time seems to stand still and the creative process you are involved in is like therapy for the soul.

See if you can get into a state of flow by doing an activity you are passionate about, such as video editing, coding a website, painting your house, working in the garden, spring cleaning, or anything else you like to do. You aren't likely to experience flow if you are constantly doing things for others or neglecting your needs so make yourself a priority and grow from this useful experience.

4. Resilience vs. Helplessness

After going through hard times, it is common for people to feel helpless in their present life. This is known as *learned helplessness* which conditions us to expect and accept pain, believing we cannot escape from it.

One of the principles of self-love is believing that you ARE entitled to live a pain-free life and that you do NOT deserve to suffer. By recognizing your self-worth, you can begin to let go of the idea that you aren't in control. As you identify your strengths and define your values, it is possible to become more resilient and overcome negative situations much more efficiently.

Instead of being helpless, you will feel that you are in the driving seat and do not need to accept anything that is harmful or unhealthy for you. This takes time and a commitment to wanting to change the way you have been living but once you embrace the idea, you will begin to see that you can control your life in a healthy, positive way.

When you love yourself deeply, you can move on from painful situations and handle life's challenges with greater success. This is because you will have covered all your bases – self-esteem, self-worth, and self-care. We are all entitled to lead full, meaningful lives and enjoy the five basic attributes of well-being that you will find below. Take a look and ask yourself how close you are to achieving each attribute – a little, somewhat, or a lot:

- Positive emotions – such as pleasure, inspiration, hope, compassion, and gratitude.
- Engagement –when you feel fully engaged in your life and experience moments of flow.
- Relationships – enjoying strong connections with others yet remaining independent.
- Meaning - when you feel connected to something larger than yourself and your life has purpose
- Accomplishments/achievements – when you feel happy about the things you have achieved or made improvements to your life.

Perhaps you feel OK sometimes, and despise yourself at other times. It is normal to have good and bad days – we all do. On your journey to nurturing more self-love, keeping a check on your emotions can be a great tool to see how well you are healing from a painful past and learning to love yourself more. Your emotional wellness relates to how good you are at recognizing, accepting, and managing your feelings every day. By measuring it, you may be able to improve it and as you practice a more emotionally healthy lifestyle, you will find that you can cope better when problems arise. The Emotional Wellness Checklist you will find below is a good way to do this and you can come back to it time after time to see how you are getting on.

Have you recently felt any of the following emotions?:

1. Contentment
2. Fear
3. Love
4. Joy
5. Depression
6. Anger
7. Interest
8. Positivity
9. Sadness
10. Pleasantness
11. Negativity
12. Happiness
13. Stress
14. Resentment
15. Vitality

Now try to answer the following questions:

1. Are you surprised by any of your responses?
2. Which feelings in particular stand out?
3. Are there any pleasant emotions you experience less frequently than you thought?
4. Do you feel any negative feelings more than you had realized?

5. What could you do to experience them less often?
6. Can you think of any specific steps you need to take to do so?

When you pay attention to your emotions, you become more in tune with your inner needs. Feeling negative is bad for your psychological and physical health so understanding what triggers that is a way to prevent it from happening more frequently. On the other hand, the more positive emotions you experience, the more self-love you will nurture.

Practicing self-love

Self-love is like a cure for feelings of negativity, pessimism, and feeling bad about life in general. It instills you with an appreciation for who you are and supports your psychological and spiritual growth. To achieve it, you can apply some practical steps that hopefully will form new habits. It's time to say goodbye to negative self-talk and welcome a new you - someone who loves yourself to the core.

Practice mindfulness. As I mentioned in the previous chapter, mindfulness is an opportunity for you to slow down and tune in to how you are feeling, as well as what you are thinking, at any given moment. It helps to release negative thoughts and allows you to gain increased self-awareness.

Nourish your mind and body. No one can deny the benefits of exercising regularly and eating a balanced diet. Getting quality sleep is also paramount as it helps the brain to reboot while you rest. Do stretching exercises when you wake in the morning, have daily walks, sit in the sun for ten minutes, and eat healthy, fresh produce every day. Reduce your caffeine intake and the amount of processed foods or alcohol you consume – you will notice the difference in no time at all.

Set your boundaries. People may ask a lot of you and expect you to always say yes to their requests. While it is nice to be of help to others, if this infringes on your time and drains your energy, you must draw the line somewhere. When you really want to say, 'No', to someone, simply explain that you are unable to accommodate them without feeling the need to explain why. Those who respect you will not be offended and those who are put out do not have your best interests at heart.

Practice self-care. Take the time to look after your appearance and your personal hygiene. Make an effort to have a regular massage, pedicure, haircut, or anything else you enjoy, and treat yourself to some new clothes if you can afford it. Not only will you look great, but the revamp will do wonders for your self-esteem. Self-care also involves listening to your emotions and honoring them. If you feel hurt by someone, allow that pain to manifest itself and then let it leave your system. Holding on to it is toxic and will do you harm. Feel, then release, to restore your inner harmony.

Look after your emotions. Dedicate a part of your day solely to meeting your needs, whether that is having a break or doing something nice because you deserve it. Congratulate yourself when you complete a task and allow yourself to feel proud. Express your emotions when they arise as long as you do it in a way that will not cause harm to others. It is perfectly OK to tell someone that you feel angry with them and to give the reasons why. Not only do you show them that you have feelings and limits, but by getting things off your chest, you will also be able to let them go and feel better afterward.

Cultivate your social life. Try to meet up with friends and family as often as possible and get out of the house more. Keep company with people who support you and stay away from those who bring you down. Talk to a trusted friend about your problems or join a support group to connect with people going through the same issues as yourself. Interacting with people more frequently can bring you a lot of joy and prevent you from feeling socially isolated. It also helps you to experience the fun side of life and you deserve to enjoy that.

Take care of your spiritual needs. No matter what your beliefs are about life and the universe, tending to your spiritual needs will fortify your sense of wholeness. We all want to feel that our life has meaning and purpose, which is why nurturing your spiritual side can bring such peace and contentment.

Pray if it brings you solace, meditate if you seek calmness, or walk in nature if you want to reconnect with the universe. You may even wish to be of service to others and this can be a wonderful way to elevate your feelings of worthiness and self-esteem. Follow your heart's desires and seek experiences that fill you with sheer awe and wonder whenever you can.

Love yourself deeply

Self-love should be your number one priority and the sooner you introduce habits into your daily life to reinforce that, the better. Here are some for you to adopt:

- Look in the mirror and tell yourself, 'I love you,' at least once a day. It might sound silly but, often, we really need to hear those words in order to believe we are worthy of love.
- Be someone who is open to love, even if you have been hurt in the past. We have an infinite capacity to love, and loving others can bring us great inner satisfaction. Love others unconditionally without expecting anything in return and notice how full you feel by doing so. Love can complete us and make us feel truly whole so go out and share it with someone today!
- Bring to mind someone that you know loves you unconditionally. It could be a parent or other family member, a partner, a friend, or anyone else in your life. Think about why they love you and hold on to that warm feeling of being loved for the special person you are.
- Tune out negative self-talk when it begins and replace it with a positive inner dialogue that focuses on your strengths and qualities. When the little voice inside your head starts telling you how worthless, useless, and unlovable you are, turn down the volume and tell yourself you are worthy, capable, and lovable, because you are!
- Accept your imperfections and don't dwell on them for too long. Self-love includes recognizing your faults and being OK with them while having the desire to improve if you can. If you cannot, that does not make you any less valuable as a

person and you don't need to torture yourself for not being perfect – none of us are.
- Let the past go – you don't need it anymore. As I've mentioned throughout this book, holding on to the weight of past events will prevent you from flourishing, so release your hold on it and look forward to a future of your own making. It is in your hands.

Write yourself a love letter

If you do not love yourself, how can you expect anyone else to love you? Deep inside, we all need to feel loved and by cultivating more self-love, you will find that life can be beautiful.

Pain and hurt can be replaced by happiness and joy when you bring more love into your life and one way to initiate that is by writing yourself a love letter. It might sound odd to do so, but the process can be very empowering and therapeutic.

All you need is a pen and paper or a notebook. You can even write it on a document on your PC, laptop, or phone. This is your chance to affirm your self-love and express appreciation for the compassionate person you are.

In your letter, you can express your thoughts and feelings, recognize your achievements, and give yourself encouragement. You can tell yourself why you are worthy, valuable, and precious – things you may not often hear from others.

Writing your letter will bring you a great sense of satisfaction and help to reinforce qualities that you may have felt lacking in. It is a genuine testament to the love you have for your well-being and happiness so please try it and see how you feel afterward.

Find some quiet time when you won't be disturbed to write your letter. It doesn't have to be very long—one or two paragraphs will do—and write from the heart. It can begin with something like this:

Dear (your name),

I want to tell you how I feel about you...

Address yourself with tenderness and empathy, allowing yourself to free up all those feelings that you have been keeping inside. Imagine it is a letter to a lover or someone who means the world to you and let the words flow...

Here is an example of a love letter I wrote to myself to give you some ideas. You don't need to be restricted by this and can write whatever you want to, but keep it positive, personal, and compassionate.

Dear Rebecca,

It's been so long since I had a chance to tell you how I feel about you and I apologize for that.

You might have thought I had forgotten about you or didn't care about you anymore. Nothing could be further from the truth. You mean everything to me and from now on I am going to tell you that more often.

I know life hasn't always been easy for you and yet, you have managed to overcome so many obstacles and achieve things not even you thought were possible. I put it down to your strength and courage, even though you always found it hard to believe in yourself. But, you should because you have come a long way since the time when you were a timid little kid. Now you are a fully-grown adult with so much to offer.

I wish you could see yourself the way I do: a strong, independent woman who is loved by so many people. Your kindness and compassion for others always amazes me, even though you remain humble and never ask for any thanks in return. I sincerely hope that you recognize how special you are and continue to pursue your dreams because you deserve to fly high.

I will always love you with all my heart.

R.

Self-love is about nurturing your inner needs and living life to the full. It might be a work in progress but if you keep applying the strategies you found in this chapter, you will eventually achieve it. I wish you well and remember to love yourself deeply every minute of the day.

Key highlights

- **Self-love is the key to freeing yourself from a life of unhappiness.**
- **Everyone deserves to be loved, regardless of their past.**
- **You can nurture more self-love by recognizing your inner worth and value.**
- **Increase your levels of self-esteem by introducing new ways of thinking and adopting new habits.**
- **Positive psychology can help you to focus on developing resilience, contentment, and emotional growth.**
- **Writing a love letter to yourself is an empowering exercise in self-love.**

AFTERWORD

"Write the bad things that are done to you in sand, but write the good things that happen to you on a piece of marble." –Arabic proverb

If our bad memories were written in sand, they would disappear as soon as the desert winds blew. It's a charming thought but, unfortunately, not so easy to accomplish in real life. They tend to follow us instead, and we allow them to because they make us feel connected to our past.

We even believe that our memories make us who we are today and that without them, we would be lost. Instead of carving good memories onto our hearts, we cling to the tangled, knotted thread of bad memories that tethers us like a prisoner to the past.

Despite that, I have endeavored to give you a lot of strategies in this book to help you unravel yourself and be free of those painful memories so you can move on to a brighter future.

Sometimes, forgetting can seem impossible and my advice has been not to waste any more energy trying to do that. Instead, I have provided ways for you to accept the past, appreciate the present, and look forward to better days to come.

We have all experienced pain and hurt at some point in our lives and many of us have also suffered serious trauma or suffering. Hopefully, through the chapters in this book, you will find ways to gradually heal and come to a place of forgiveness.

You may be carrying the weight of past events on your shoulders and feel unable to shed the load. Perhaps you find it difficult to do because it means letting go of something that feels all too familiar. Maybe you are fearful of moving on and staying where you are seems like a safer option, even if that is not good for your mental, physical or emotional well-being.

Whatever the reasons for your inability to let go of the past until now, I sincerely hope that this book has brought you some insights into how you can relieve yourself of the emotional burden you have been carrying for so long. You will have read some of the reasons why we find it hard to let go and discovered ways to untangle the past from your present.

I have also dedicated a lot of time within these pages explaining the importance of forgiveness, which I know can seem so hard to do when you have been wronged. Hopefully, you will take my advice onboard about how to deal with painful memories and begin to implement my strategies for disarming them when they arise.

I am sure you will find the practical tips on how to stop focusing on the past very helpful and can begin to incorporate them into your daily routine.

I have talked about the mind-body dynamic in relation to trauma and given you some useful tools to use to help the healing process, including an action plan on how to release trapped emotions. As for emotional triggers, you can use the strategies I have included to help you identify and manage them when they are activated.

Forgiving and forgetting is a difficult process to go through but I hope you have gained an understanding of why both are so important to your overall well-being. You will even find a forgiveness contract included that will allow you to leave your demons behind. After all, forgiveness is about healing your inner turmoil and finding peace, which brings closure and an end to suffering.

Finally, I've given you guidance on how to start making new, positive memories to replace the negative ones from the past. It's all about spending your time with the people who make you happy, doing the things that bring you joy and being in the places that bring you peace.

Making new memories is much better than being stuck in the past and they will become a rich store of happy moments that you can retrieve in the future.

As we reach the end of this book, I would like you to make a declaration to yourself – a commitment to letting go and moving forward. There is no better time to do that than now so take a deep breath and shout as loud as you can:

'My past is gone. I choose to live in the now and a bright future awaits me.'

Well done!

You are on your way and I wish you all the best.

Rebecca

Could I ask you a favour?. would you spare 2 minutes to write an honest review for this book from wherever you bought it. Reviews mean such a lot to me. Thanks in advance.

Rebecca x

Other Books By Rebecca Collins

Love Yourself Like A Man

Love Yourself Deeply

How To Make Friends Easily

Love Yourself Deeply & How To Make Friends Easily 2 in 1 Book

The Art Of Manifesting Money

Help!, I'm a Teenager

Positive Life Skills For Teens

SOURCES

https://www.researchgate.net/publication/287000336_The_efficacy_of_forgiveness_intervention_in_college_age_adults_Randomized_controlled_study

https://www.cell.com/current-biology/fulltext/S0960-9822(21)01284-7?_returnURL=https%3A%2F%2Flinkinghub.elsevier.com%2Fretrieve%2Fpii%2FS0960982221012847%3Fshowall%3Dtrue

Hanson, R., Hardwiring Happiness: The New Brain Science of Contentment, Calm, and Confidence, Harmony 2013

https://www.ncbi.nlm.nih.gov/books/NBK207191/

Van der Kolk, B. A., The Body Keeps the Score: Mind and Body in the Healing of Trauma, Penguin 2015

https://psycnet.apa.org/doiLanding?doi=10.1037%2Fa0035268

http://abcnews.go.com/US/york-woman-blinded-shopping-cart-dropped-teens-forgives/story?id=15959174

My Book

https://www.verywellmind.com/martin-seligman-biography-2795527

NOTES

2. THE ART OF FORGIVENESS

1. https://www.researchgate.net/publication/287000336_The_efficacy_of_forgiveness_intervention_in_college_age_adults_Randomized_controlled_study

3. DEALING WITH PAINFUL MEMORIES

1. https://www.cell.com/current-biology/fulltext/S0960-9822(21)01284-7?_returnURL=https%3A%2F%2Flinkinghub.elsevier.com%2Fretrieve%2Fpii%2FS0960982221012847%3Fshowall%3Dtrue
2. Hanson, R., Hardwiring Happiness: The New Brain Science of Contentment, Calm, and Confidence, Harmony 2013
3. https://www.ncbi.nlm.nih.gov/books/NBK207191/

4. THE MIND-BODY DYNAMIC

1. Van der Kolk, B. A., The Body Keeps the Score: Mind and Body in the Healing of Trauma, Penguin 2015

6. FORGIVE AND MOVE ON

1. https://psycnet.apa.org/doiLanding?doi=10.1037%2Fa0035268
2. http://abcnews.go.com/US/york-woman-blinded-shopping-cart-dropped-teens-forgives/story?id=15959174
3. https://www.amazon.com/Just-Let-Henry-Ian-Cusick/dp/B0155P1EDG

7. MOVING INTO THE LIGHT

1. Martin Seligman Biography and Psychological Theories